DR ELISABETH MARX is a Director of Norman Broadbent International, the worldwide executive search company. She focuses on the search for and psychological development of international executives and carries out research on boardroom issues. Based in London, she works throughout Europe and the United States and lectures on management topics internationally. Her work on management issues is frequently covered in the national and international press as well as on radio and television.

She trained in psychology at the University of Marburg (Germany), gained her doctorate at Oxford University, and was previously a lecturer in psychology at the National University of Singapore.

Praise for
Breaking Through Culture Shock

"The theme is upbeat. Most managers can be effective abroad if they work hard on their adaptability. The most self-aware executives appear to experience the most intense culture shock and also to adapt best.
Particularly instructive are the many case studies and interviews. This is an accessible and practical self-help book."
Financial Times

"Marx writes in a highly readable style and provides a useful combination of practical case studies and commentary. Her culture shock triangle model also benefits from an elegant simplicity ... and should guarantee the book a wide audience in both boardrooms and HR functions.
A valuable resource for HR practitioners involved in preparing and developing managers to work abroad ... this is also a highly recommended read for people currently undertaking an international assignment or working within an international team."
Bob Morton, People Management

"Practical and well-written. Recommended not only for junior and senior managers aspiring for professional success in different cultural settings, this excellent guide is also valuable reading for international business students and business academics."
CHOICE

"For anyone contemplating an international assignment or wrestling with the shock of one, this book is full of insights and practical advice on how to break through culture shock and enjoy an effective and enriching international role."
Employment Conditions Abroad

"An excellent model for developing organizational effectiveness and for managing an international career – this book provides a great combination of research, case studies and sound practical advice on how to make it in the international arena."
Richard Simmons, Senior Partner, Arthur Andersen

"Dr Marx's incisive commentary on key issues facing international managers, and by implication, multinational corporations, makes compulsive reading. Every international manager should examine the proposed psychological steps to cultural effectiveness. The book also provides chief executives and HR directors alike with a unique perspective on the challenges of developing a truly international management cadre."
Stephen Dando, Group Management Development Director, Diageo

"Refreshingly different in its holistic approach to cross-cultural, international management and candid in its presentation of the issues, *Breaking Through Culture Shock* provides some choice insights into an increasingly significant aspect of business and domestic life."
Management Skills & Development

Breaking Through Culture Shock

"This is a very well-crafted book, a 'must read' for any manager considering an international posting. Highly practical, it weaves together a substantial number of case studies and the best of academic research.

Most books on cross-cultural problems consider international managers as inanimate humanoids – to be observed, counted and categorized. Refreshingly, Elisabeth Marx does not. Her approach is anchored in what real managers feel and do and then gently and persuasively recommends achievable strategies for improving personal success. Well done!"

Professor David Norburn, Director of The Management School
Imperial College, University of London

To my parents and their inimitable way
of crossing borders

Breaking Through Culture Shock

What you need to succeed in
international business

Elisabeth Marx

NICHOLAS BREALEY
PUBLISHING

LONDON

This paperback edition first published by Nicholas Brealey Publishing in association with Intercultural Press in 2001.

Nicholas Brealey Publishing   *nbi*   Intercultural Press
36 John Street   PO Box 700
London WC1N 2AT, UK   Yarmouth, Maine 04096 USA
44-207-430-0224   001-207-846-5168
Fax: 44-207-404-8311   Fax: 001-207-846-5181
www.nbrealey-books.com   www.interculturalpress.com

First published in hardcover by Nicholas Brealey Publishing in 1999

ISBN 1-85788-220-2 (hardcover)
ISBN 1-85788-221-0 (softcover)

Printed in Finland

Library of Congress Cataloging-in-Publication Data
Marx, Elisabeth.
   Breaking through culture shock: what you need to succeed in international business/
Elizabeth Marx
         p.   cm.
   Includes bibliographical references and index.
   ISBN 1-85788-220-2   (hardcover)
   1. Corporate culture.   2. Business etiquette.   3. Culture shock.   4. Intercultural
communication.   5. Management.   6. Competition, International.   I. Title.
   HD58.7.M3747   1999
   658—dc21   98–46502
                                                                                          CIP
British Library Cataloguing in Publication Data
A catalogue record for this book is available from the British Library.

Substantial discounts on bulk quantities are available. For details, discount information, or to request a free catalogue, please contact the publishers at the addresses given above.

Contents

Acknowledgments

Many inspiring individuals and organizations have supported this project and contributed to its implementation. I am extremely grateful for all the help I have received throughout. In particular, I would like to thank:

▲ Peter Job of Reuters, Win Bischoff of Schroders, Edward Dolman of Christie's, David John of BOC, Caroline Kuhnert of Warburg Dillon Read and Deborah Percy of Blockbuster for giving me their valuable time and for allowing me to use their experiences as case studies of successful international executives.
▲ David Ellison of the Centre for International Briefing for collaborating on one of the research projects and for always showing interest in my ideas.
▲ Annabel Hendry of the Foreign Office for her input on the partner issue.
▲ Dr Chua Fook Kee of the National University of Singapore for cutting to the chase and for his clear ideas on language and thinking.
▲ Associate Professor Chang Weining of the National University of Singapore for discussions on identity and on paradigm shift in warmer climates.
▲ My brother, Dr Michael Marx of the University of Heidelberg, for his medical recommendations regarding working in tropical countries.
▲ Clare Harrison of HCR World Connect for allowing me to use her relocation checklist.

▲ Norman Broadbent International for giving me the scope to carry out research projects on management issues. I am especially grateful to Gary Luddington, the Chairman of NBI, for his support and to my colleagues James Hervey-Bathurst and Jerry Gray for their exceptional interest and input in my work.

▲ Rachel Boyd for her excellent administrative and secretarial help and for her spirited approach throughout.

▲ Nicholas Brealey for helping me to shape the topic in a significant and creative way and for his perseverance in showing me that my ideas are not always the best – he is a great inspiration for any management writer.

▲ Sally Lansdell, my editor, for her genius in turning my Germanic writing into English prose and for her great understanding of what I am trying to say.

▲ The Anglo-German Foundation for funding my research project on international human resource practices in Germany. I am particularly grateful to Dr Ray Cunningham.

▲ The HR directors of over 200 international organizations who were contacted at various points in the project to participate in surveys.

▲ My family and friends for encouraging me to take on new endeavors and for being supportive throughout.

▲ Finally, all the international executives who were so generous with their time in talking to me and who were inspirational in leading interesting and enriched lives – without their help, this book would not have been possible.

Preface to the Paperback Edition

What makes some international managers highly successful whereas others struggle with basic everyday activities? If we are all so 'global' nowadays, what makes some of us more international than others? It's not the number of airmiles we clock up on transatlantic flights, nor is it the technical excellence we bring to our jobs. In my experience, it is our ability to manage culture shock in international business that makes the difference between failure and success.

Culture shock – the experience of foreignness – is an 'occupational hazard' (and opportunity) in today's global business. Whereas some executives clearly thrive on this challenge, others feel disoriented and anxious and do not perform well. It is estimated that one in seven UK managers fail on international assignments and this figure is even higher for US managers, with an estimated failure rate of 25–40 percent. Some managers seem to adapt in an almost chameleon-like way to different countries, whereas others cling desperately to their habits and their national approaches.

A recent survey of 500 multinational firms in the US showed that nearly 29 percent of international assignees are now on short-term assignments. Virtual expatriate assignments seem to be an increasing trend, with executives working overseas but not living overseas.

But how exactly does culture shock show itself and what do you need to make it in the international arena? Whether on short- or long-term assignments, you have to recognize and deal with three areas where culture shock could affect you:

▲ *Emotions*: you have to cope with the stress of international work and keep an emotional balance in order to perform in a business.
▲ *Thinking style*: you have to understand how your counterparts think and be able to develop culturally effective solutions.
▲ *Social skills and social identity*: you need effective social skills to establish new business relationships.

The basic assumption of this book is that effective international managers are not born but made, i.e. you have to work at it, but by managing the elements of the culture shock triangle you can achieve international effectiveness. The only managers who can be called truly international are those who understand themselves and develop as emotional, thinking and social beings – you need to have a good level of self-understanding before you can understand your foreign counterparts.

This book is a self-coaching guide for managers working in an international setting, whether away from their own country or in a multinational organization. It will take you step by step through what you need to succeed. Not something to be read passively or in the bath, it addresses three areas to which you should take an active approach:

▲ *Self-development*: How can you adapt effectively to the requirements of international work?
▲ *Cross-cultural development*: How can you understand foreign counterparts better or motivate an international team?
▲ *Career development*: How should you manage your international career in the long run?

The idea for this book developed out of my own experiences of culture shock. As a German psychologist, I experienced my first major culture shock when I came to Britain for my postgraduate studies. This sparked my interest in both cross-cultural adaptation and cross-cultural psychology, an interest I could pursue while working in Singapore before coming to London to work with international managers. I decided not to rely on anecdotes but instead to take a scientific approach and find out systematically what international managers experience on their assignments as well as what their organizations do to help them. The results of my research showed massive gaps or, to put it more positively, room for improvement. It became obvious that many organizations do not prepare their managers sufficiently for working abroad. However, it was also evident that ambitious managers have to be proactive in managing their career and their self-development.

This book will help you to achieve exactly this kind of self-development. The first part of the book looks at the psychological concepts of international effectiveness. Chapter 1 explains the concept of culture shock and sets the scene for managing the three areas of the culture shock triangle: emotions, thinking and social skills and identity. This triangle is described in detail in Chapters 2, 3 and 4, together with clear coping strategies and suggestions on how to succeed. There are checklists and exercises to help you think about the issues in a practical way, together with a new framework for understanding cross-cultural differences.

The second part of the book focuses on the steps towards a successful international career. Chapter 5 summarizes the characteristics of some of the world's main business cultures. Chapter 6 addresses your personal life, including dual-career issues and children. Chapter 7 gives suggestions on managing your international career, short term and long term. Chapter 8 summarizes the lessons for multinational organizations, and Chapter 9 provides the view of global leaders. Chapter 10 concludes with an evaluation of your own abilities to succeed internationally.

The paperback edition of the book also focuses on the increasing trend to virtual international work and includes a section on the development of virtual teams.

My own outlook is straightforward: working internationally is difficult, challenging and can be extremely exhilarating. At times a frustrating experience, it is never boring and it will enrich your personal and professional life if you approach it in the right way. I hope this book will help you to do just that.

Part One

Experiencing Culture Shock – Learning to Adapt

1

The Culture Shock Triangle

Imagine that you have just come back from a meeting with your boss. Your job has been going extremely well and you had great expectations before your discussion. These were more than surpassed when you were offered an international role, either a foreign assignment or a short-term international project. This is exactly what you wanted. You are ambitious and you know that if you want to succeed, you need the international experience.

At the same time, your exhilaration is slightly dampened by uncertainty about how you are going to adapt, how this change will affect your personal life and how you will be able to develop quickly in the international arena.

The future you envisage will depend to a great extent on your personality. If you are an optimist, you will probably picture an ideal scenario and identify with this international executive:

"I always wanted to work abroad; I left university and wanted to go and see the world – work hard and play hard. The oil industry seemed ideal for this purpose. I saw myself as a nomad since I left my home country when I was 11 years old to do my

education abroad. I worked in a number of countries, often with very little organizational support. I started my first assignment in my early twenties and developed a flexibility and an understanding of what others do. The most important factor was having an easy-going personality. As a consequence of long-term international work, I feel I am able to see things from many angles and I regard it as a particularly broadening experience. **"**

This is the way we all like to see ourselves: an early international orientation, a flexible and easy-going personality, an ability to look at situations from different perspectives and a high degree of tolerance.

However, if you are more of a pessimist, you may envisage something similar to the following scenario:

"My *adaptation was appallingly difficult. I thought I knew the French, but I only knew them socially and not in a working environment. The French manager had been fired but he had recruited all of the French employees and so the French employees thought that the manager was badly treated. I found that all the normal ways of managing people in the UK did not work in France. The things I said were not perceived the way I intended and, in turn, I did not understand exactly what they were saying. What I found was a lot of bad will. At first, I tried to charm them and in the end I had to get rid of them. It took 18 months to sort out the situation and it was only really resolved after my car tires were slashed and it was in a way an attempt at murder. I was driving with my family at high speed for 100 km before I noticed because of the way they were slashed. What really helped me was having a strong outside interest and strong religious beliefs.* **"**

Or there is an even more pessimistic scenario:

"I *was a 45-year-old American and had come to Asia to work on a three-year assignment. Although I saw myself as a very sociable and adaptable man, my work pattern became erratic, which was noted by my company. I would be late and sometimes not turn up at all – at other times, I seemed to work around the clock.*

My colleagues seemed to be used to the 'eccentric' behavior of for-
eigners and did not think too much about it.

After six months, I fetched a boat to an island in a neighboring
country; on arrival, I took off my clothes, and threatened the local
population with a gun in a stark-naked state. Eventually, I suc-
cumbed to the police and was brought back to my home country. It
was clear that I could not stay abroad and function in my job – I
returned 'home to recover'. "

All three examples are from real life. They are accounts by Italian,
British and American international managers who are well educated
and in senior positions, working in different parts of the world. All
were confronted with the same basic challenge: being effective at an
international level and adapting to a new culture. The scenarios show
a range of effects that foreign encounters can have: from exhilaration
and developing confidence to serious intercultural problems and even
the worst-case scenario of a 'nervous breakdown'.

Fortunately, most international managers experience a mixture of
these scenarios: they go through some difficult phases but eventually
develop effective international skills.

The basic proposition of this book is a positive one: the majority of
us can be internationally effective if we put real effort into developing
our ability to adapt. In the past, most books on international managers
have concentrated on specific aspects of intercultural work, with a
particular focus on understanding the cultural dimensions of management. This is obviously necessary, but it isn't sufficient – it doesn't
look at the international manager as a human being with development
needs at a professional *and* personal level. We need to think differently
in a new culture, but we also have to adapt to the challenge socially
and emotionally.

Culture shock

Working in a new culture can produce a variety of reactions, such as:

▲ Confusion about what to do
▲ Anxiety
▲ Frustration
▲ Exhilaration
▲ Inappropriate social behavior
▲ Inability to get close to your business partner and clinch the deal
▲ Feeling isolated
▲ Becoming depressed.

All of these are possible reactions to culture shock, the shock we experience when we are confronted with the unknown and the 'foreign'. The term 'culture shock', now part of our everyday vocabulary, was coined by the anthropologist Oberg (1960), who explained both the symptoms and the process of adapting to a different culture. The experience of a new culture is seen as an unpleasant surprise or shock – a shock that occurs when expectations do not coincide with reality.

In his original article, Oberg lists six main aspects of culture shock:

▲ *Strain* caused by the effort to adapt
▲ *Sense of loss and feelings of deprivation* in relation to friends, status, profession and possessions
▲ *Feeling rejected* by or rejecting members of the new culture
▲ *Confusion* in role, values and self-identity
▲ *Anxiety and even disgust/anger* about 'foreign' practices
▲ *Feelings of helplessness*, not being able to cope with the new environment.

It is a myth that experiencing culture shock is a weakness or a negative indication of future international success. Culture shock in all its diverse forms is completely normal and is part of a successful process of adaptation. A study of Canadian expatriates in Africa showed that those who experienced culture shock were ultimately the most effective (Hawes and Kealey, 1981). Expatriates who were most aware of themselves and their emotions experienced the most intense culture shock, but it was exactly because of this intense awareness of differences that they were also able to adapt more effectively later on.

In contrast, expatriates who were not affected by culture shock and generalized their own views to the other culture did not adapt very well. Culture shock is therefore a positive sign on the road to international adaptation.

Symptoms of culture shock

Although we use the term culture shock all the time, there is very little information on its most frequent symptoms and the degree to which managers experience them. This is an area I looked at in conjunction with the UK's Centre for International Briefing (Marx, 1998).

We asked 73 managers who worked all over the world to complete a questionnaire in the first six months of their international assignments. The majority were in fairly senior positions, typically regional directors within a functional area.

The following examples show different experiences of culture shock.

"Culture shock – still going on after five weeks here." (A *manager in Indonesia who reported symptoms including feelings of isolation, anxiety, helplessness and performance deficit*)

"Experienced symptoms from month three to six. I accepted that it would happen and worked through it." (A manager in Poland)

"The culture shock lasted about three to four months; the only way out was to remind myself of what I had achieved in previous jobs under difficult circumstances and set myself achievement targets on a daily and weekly basis." (A manager working in Russia taking a very structured approach)

How long does culture shock last?

Most people think of culture shock as a 'short and sharp', disorientating experience in a foreign place. Few realize that its effects can be much deeper and more prolonged if it is not dealt with effectively.

On average, managers in my study experienced culture shock symptoms for about seven weeks: 70 percent of managers reported these lasting up to five weeks and 30 percent had symptoms for up to ten weeks.

In order of priority, the symptoms most often found were:

▲ feeling isolated
▲ anxiety and worry
▲ reduction in job performance
▲ high energy
▲ helplessness.

The inclusion of 'high energy' may be surprising, but it could be nervous energy, or a high energy level caused by changing circumstances, possibly those involved in the adaptation process. The longer the international manager experienced culture shock, the greater were the feelings of helplessness and performance deficit. This suggests that not coping with culture shock symptoms when they appear can lead to a very negative situation.

Phases of adaptation

Oberg developed a model of adaptation that suggests that going abroad or working internationally puts you through a cycle of distinct phases on the way to final adaptation.

The first stage is the *honeymoon phase*, where all encounters in the new place are seen as exciting, positive and stimulating. The new life is viewed as providing endless opportunities and the manager is usually in a state of exhilaration. There is openness and curiosity, combined with a readiness to accept whatever comes. Most importantly, at this stage judgment is reserved and even minor irritations are suppressed in favor of concentrating on the nice things about the job, the country, the colleagues, the food, etc.

In the second phase, *culture shock* sets in – the manager realizes that something is not quite right. This experience of foreignness can start with a creeping awareness of disorientation and a feeling of not quite knowing what is going on. It can also include very negative symptoms, such as stress (being unable to sleep or eat), irritability, a negative view of the job, the country and colleagues.

This phase is characterized by a general unease that can involve being uncomfortable with the new situation but can border on hating everything foreign. The main reason for these symptoms is an uncertainty about ourselves, our surroundings and our future. The usual signs of orientation and belonging do not exist, we don't quite know who we are without the familiar social context, and the way our foreign colleagues behave seems 'all wrong'.

How individual managers deal with this particular phase and its emotions, thinking and expectations is essential for their overall adaptation in the long run. The ideal approach is to use the symptoms and the unpleasantness as a clear indicator that it is time to change our approach and to engage in some form of self-development – both in dealing with our emotions and in understanding ourselves and others. The worst type of approach is to ignore the symptoms, to resort to superficial solutions (including the long-term use of tranquilizers) or to adapt a rigid stance of believing that only our own methods are correct and forcing these methods/management techniques on foreign colleagues.

The third phase of *recovery* usually starts with accepting that we have a problem and that we have to work on it. Both recovery and the final adjustment phase usually involve a compromise between the feeling and thinking of the honeymoon phase and the culture shock phase. This compromise is between our exaggerated expectations and reality. In the final, *adjustment* stage, managers are able to work effectively, know the limitations of their skills, can take on new ways of doing things and, most importantly, are able to be more flexible.

Figure 1 shows the adaptation phases and the mood changes involved. We could obviously apply these phases to different life events, such as taking on a new job, marriage, or even buying a house. The first stage always involves excitement, euphoria and optimism – the 'honeymoon'. The second stage is a confrontation with the

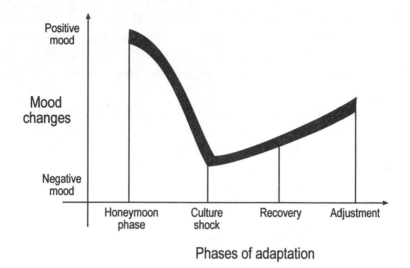

Figure 1 Stages of adaptation (after Oberg, 1960)

unknown and the negative aspects of the event: confusion, anxiety and frustration set in. At some point, we recover from the depression and anxiety of culture shock and, in the fourth and final stage, we head for a readjustment.

As one female US manager remarked:

> " *It was in the seventh or eighth month that I clearly was having symptoms of culture shock: I was confused, annoyed, I asked questions like: 'Why are the banks not better?' I was looking at identifying all the inefficiencies of the British system. I hated the British business culture which I saw as slow, bureaucratic, cumbersome, lacking customer service, lacking initiatives. Fortunately, I had a very good mentor and I could go on Friday afternoons and moan and talk to him about my experiences. I was able to make a much better adjustment, and after about 12 months I felt integrated and also reconciled. I had counseling during this period and one of the most helpful things was that the counselor explained the phases of adaptation. This made clear that my experiences, which were sometimes very negative, were part of a normal pattern.* "

Most managers who have spent some time abroad agree with this model of adaptation. Most of those I interviewed described their excitement and curiosity at the beginning, the feelings of well-being and optimism; however, they also recalled times when they felt stressed and socially isolated.

Many experts have tried to specify the timings of these different phases or, in other words, to define what is 'normal' in adapting to a foreign culture. However, there is no hard-and-fast rule. In my view, the timing of culture shock will depend on the 'foreignness' of the culture (how different it is to your own culture), the social context (whether you have support through an expatriate network or through host-country nationals) and the personality of the international manager involved. These phases of culture shock may not always appear in such a neat sequence.

It is more realistic to use a model of culture shock that is not strictly linear but integrates a dynamic and repetitive cycle of positive and negative phases until you break through the culture shock, as in Figure 2.

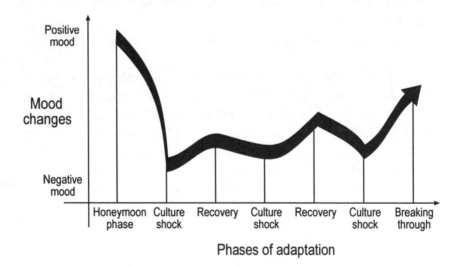

Figure 2 Breaking through culture shock

A German manager working in Africa remarked:

"I had a very negative phase after the first year. I cannot see clearly defined stages that run in a linear fashion as described in the original culture shock model. It is more like a lot of ups and downs and maybe something like a mini repetition of the culture shock cycle throughout one's stay abroad. The way I coped with my own emotions was to talk to someone close about it. "

Short-term assignments

International assignments now tend to be shorter (consistent with the trend in multinational organizations to abolish the term 'expatriates'). There are more executives working on short-term international projects and there are even more managers who work in international teams from their home base.

Does the same culture shock model apply to international managers on shorter-term assignments or remaining in their home country with frequent international trips? I believe that the same concept applies but that a different model is warranted. Obviously, short-term international work does not allow for the same long-term adaptation process and therefore distinct honeymoon, culture shock and readjustment phases will not occur. Instead, there will be more of a mixture of positive and negative emotions, of uncertainty and clarity, of enjoyment and frustration.

Although a different model applies, the same components are involved in adapting to short-term international work. The same experience of the unknown is present and similar reactions to personal issues and management situations will therefore occur.

The culture shock triangle

The culture shock model we have discussed so far mainly focuses on the emotional consequences of international encounters (positive and negative), the potential stress involved and the ultimate adjustment to reach contentment. However, some of the symptoms that Oberg lists show different aspects of culture shock, such as confusion about roles and values or disorientation when confronted with 'foreign' practices. In order to boost our international effectiveness, we need to consider *all* levels of culture shock within a more comprehensive model.

Psychologically, international managers have to deal with three levels of culture shock:

▲ Emotions – coping with mood swings
▲ Thinking – understanding foreign colleagues
▲ Social skills and identity – developing a social and professional
  network and effective social skills.

This leads to a new model of culture shock – the *culture shock triangle* (see Figure 3).

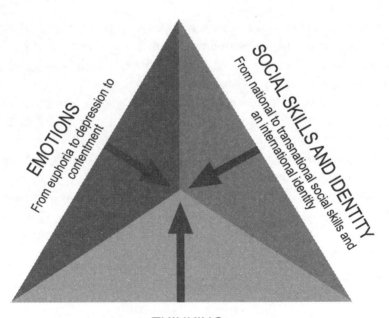

THINKING
From stereotyping to culturally effective thinking

Figure 3 The culture shock triangle

Questions every international manager should ask include:

▲ *Emotions* – What am I likely to feel? How will I cope with the stress of international work?
▲ *Thinking* – What will I think? How good are my business solutions?
▲ *Social skills and identity* – How effectively will I interact with my foreign counterparts?

These three levels of international adaptation lead to the following aims for managers:

▲ Coping with the stress of the transition (achieving contentment).
▲ Changing the perception and interpretation of events and behavior (developing a way of thinking that is culturally effective).
▲ Developing better social skills and an international identity.

These three aims combine to form the culture shock triangle, achieving the international effectiveness on which this book focuses.

Although they are treated as distinct components, they are, of course, interrelated and influence each other. For example, 'feeling irritated' has a negative effect on thinking as well as on social behavior. If you are pessimistic and stressed out, your solutions to problems are likely to be rigid and therefore ineffective. Socially, you may be withdrawn or unable to achieve rapport with others. In contrast, a positive mood and optimism produce better solutions.

The way we think and behave also influences our emotions. If you are passive and withdrawn, you are less likely to get positive feedback from others which, in turn, will make you feel low.

Emotions

International executives often report the positive effects of their work on their personality, but they also mention emotional reactions, such as worry, feelings of isolation and helplessness.

One example of an extreme reaction was reported by a western manager in Shanghai:

" *Culture shock – continuous feeling of being unwell due to two bouts of bad food poisoning – loneliness, most prominent was the constant staring from the Chinese. This curiosity became very upsetting – everything in my hotel room was looked through, all drawers in my desk searched through. Also, telephone conversations were tapped, I could hear the click and the echo which does not happen now. This led to continuous paranoia. To resolve this, I eventually managed to relax and to take no notice, I pretended it did not happen and, most importantly, every three to four weeks I left China to visit other countries such as Japan, Korea and Hawaii.*

Another culture shock was the physical adaptation to the pollution and the stinging eyes, the sheer noise of cars and people. I think only the World Health Organisation could resolve that!

I also felt helpless – I was deported once for not having a correct visa and had an overnight stay in a state-run guesthouse with a government immigration official. So why am I here? Because it is a good career move (hopefully) for the future. "

Moving to a foreign country means stress for the individual and international assignments fall into the category of stressful 'life events' (Furnham and Bochner, 1986). These are major life changes that put the individual at risk of psychological difficulties, such as depression, anxiety, alcoholism or what is typically called a 'nervous breakdown'. Psychological research has shown that there is a link between the number of life events suffered (such as changing jobs, divorce, bereavement) and psychological disorders (Dohrenwend and Dohrenwend, 1974). International managers who move abroad experience several such events: changing country, changing job and changing house. Consequently, there is a high risk to their psychological well-being and hence a high risk of performance deficits at work – and, ultimately, a risk for the company.

Moreover, these changes affect the entire family. Spouses often give up their jobs without any prospect of finding equivalent employment abroad. Children are uprooted and have to cope with new schools and a whole new environment.

These changes are not restricted to managers who embark on longer-term international assignments. Dealing with new environments, a hectic lifestyle and constant traveling can produce similar effects in the 'short-term' international manager.

Thinking

Living in a familiar, well-structured and predictable environment makes understanding easy. The meaning of expressions, gestures and cultural norms is clear. We can decipher them on autopilot. If someone greets us with 'How are you?', we usually assume it is meant in a friendly way and we answer 'Fine, thank you'. But even moving to another, maybe remote, part of the same country changes that status. For example, 'How are you?' may simply mean 'Hello' and not require a reply about how we are feeling. We cannot take things for granted; all of sudden, it is an effort to understand what is going on. Most importantly, we must learn new things and expand our thinking.

New situations or situations that do not automatically make sense can be treated in one of three ways:

▲ We can decide to ignore or discard them.
▲ We can decide to treat them as familiar situations, thereby potentially drawing the wrong conclusions.
▲ We can admit that we can't make sense of them and try to expand and modify our 'typical' thinking: "It's not done like this in X, but it must have a special meaning in Y; let's try to get more information, develop alternative interpretations and so challenge existing thinking and develop a new way of thinking."

The international manager has to decide how to treat the 'foreign' situation and can become one of the following:

▲ A *colonialist* – not even reacting to the foreign culture.
▲ An *imperialist* – forcing their value system and way of thinking on to the new culture, not adapting how they interact and not seeing the necessity to change their perceptions and attitude.
▲ An *internationalist/interculturalist* – someone who is fully aware of the complexity and ambiguity of exchanges in foreign cultures

and who tries to adapt by changing their thinking and attitudes and by trying to find a compromise between cultures.

Ideally, we all want to achieve the third option.

Some international managers mention the 'thinking effect' explicitly when asked about the impact of international experience on their personality:

> *"International work makes you more aware and more knowledgeable. The result is being able to see things from many different angles; it is a very broadening experience!"*

> *"The differences in attitudes were larger than I expected, but I have reached a better understanding of different attitudes towards work."*

However, we don't only have to challenge our assumptions and values – challenging our identity and social behavior is also part of building an effective international career.

Social identity and social skills

Our identity or sense of self develops in typical stages. The tumultuous teenage years of confusion and the search for our 'self' in the early twenties are, under normal circumstances, overtaken by a mature state of self-knowledge and self-acceptance – a knowledge of our personality.

This secure sense of self is disturbed by working in an 'alien' environment. The familiar context in which our behavior makes sense is missing and behavior that is rewarded and valued at home may be negatively assessed in the new culture. For example, directness and assertiveness may be positive attributes in the USA, but would be seen as rude and inadequate in China.

Unfamiliar influences can pose a risk to our self-identify: we are not as sure as before about who we are and so we feel insecure. We learn that there are different ways of living, working and establishing relationships and this threatens our well-formed notions of how to act. We don't even understand some of our own behavior or the emotional ups and downs that we are undergoing as part of our adaptation. Our self-identity is shaken up and we may have to renegotiate or redefine that identity by integrating our new experiences and reactions into our 'old self'.

As soon as we interact more closely with a foreign culture, we experience a conflict between our own values and those of that culture. There is a collision of values. As we get more and more involved, we normally develop alternative ways of behaving and this also influences our view of ourselves. This is all part of the self-development that most people go through during international assignments.

The positive effect of international work on self-development is illustrated in the following comment:

"My most positive surprise was to realize that I was a born survivor and that I could deal with problems. It was very good for my self-image and I learned that I had a lot of staying power."

Social skills: combining business and pleasure?

Germans take a structured approach to business: they negotiate in conference rooms and they may have a meal with their negotiation partners after the deal is clinched. They take a highly situation-specific approach to business – there is a clear divide between business and pleasure. Chinese businesspeople, in contrast, meet a business partner over lunch, dinner and, if the deal is really important, at home. They try to get to know the person first before any business is discussed.

Different countries have different attitudes to mixing business and pleasure. This requires individual managers to adapt to the setting of the specific country and to develop whatever social skills are required. In my experience, western managers need some time to adapt to the combined business and pleasure approach prevalent in Asian or South American countries. In particular, introvert or socially reserved managers who find it easy to work in structured business situations are at a loss at cocktail parties or dinners where the conversation is not focused on business issues but on how good their golf is. Similarly, some western business practices (North American or northern

European) may be difficult for executives who come from a more diffuse culture, such as Asia. They may find the highly structured way of doing business in the USA curt, disrespectful or even downright rude.

However, cultural adaptation goes beyond mechanistic 'dos and don'ts'. It is more important to develop attitudes and behavior that are comfortable and effective for the individual manager in the new business culture.

The three components of the culture shock triangle will be considered in detail in Chapters 2, 3 and 4.

10 steps for minimizing culture shock

This book explains how to break through culture shock by taking the following steps:

▲ Don't let culture shock take you by surprise. Allow time to find out about it before you leave for your assignment. Learn to recognize the symptoms and their potential impact.
▲ Expect culture shock to happen irrespective of location. It is as likely to occur in a country near to your home base as in postings further afield.
▲ As soon as you arrive in your new location, identify all the opportunities for building support networks with other international managers and with local people.
▲ As with any stressful situation, fight it, don't give in to it. So don't resort to escapist strategies such as drinking or eating too much and don't deny your symptoms.
▲ Ask other international managers for guidance on the issues and problems to look out for. Learn from their experience.
▲ Give yourself time to adapt and don't rush into too many work-related projects at the start of the assignment. Make sure that the organization gives you this time too.
▲ Don't hesitate to seek professional help if symptoms persist despite your coping efforts. Help may be available within your company or externally through counselors or the medical profession.

▲ Expect the same symptoms to reoccur when you come home. Reverse culture shock is normal.

▲ Think about the positive aspects of culture shock – people who experience it adapt better to their new environment than those who do not.

▲ Retain a sense of humor!

2

Balancing Your Emotions

In 1996 a book by Daniel Goleman climbed the world's bestseller lists: *Emotional Intelligence*. Combining emotions with intelligence was new – suggesting that emotional intelligence is the most important factor for success in a career and life in general was revolutionary.

In the past, psychologists and educators had focused primarily on academic intelligence: they tried to measure how academically 'smart' a person was; they tried to find out whether a teenager was good at verbal thinking or dealing with numbers, whether a manager had good analytical skills and so on. They assumed that academic intelligence would predict a person's future job success and therefore would be one of the most important areas on which to focus in both adolescence and adult life.

There have always been sceptics challenging this assumption. We all know people with few qualifications and possibly low academic intelligence who are extremely successful. There are plenty of examples of classic entrepreneurs with modest academic achievements but real brilliance in building and running companies. Moreover, psychological research has shown that academic intelligence as measured by traditional IQ tests is only a moderate predictor of success in life.

So what accounts for success? According to Goleman, the important ingredient is emotional intelligence: the ability to understand yourself and others, to be sensitive and monitor your emotions and good social skills.

Dealing with the stresses of international work and developing cross-cultural sensitivity are part of emotional intelligence. It is not just succeeding in an assignment in South America or being effective at short-term international work – it is about developing the ability to be more effective in your career and life in general. Although we will deal in this chapter with the specific emotional juggle of international work, remember that any improvements in your emotional intelligence will enhance your problem-solving and management skills.

But this chapter does not aim to be a theoretical exercise on emotional intelligence – instead, it will focus on the practical aspects of the effect of emotions in international work, with the aim of helping you to:

▲ Recognize and be aware of extreme emotions in your response to international work.
▲ Use this self-awareness to cope with potential negative emotions.
▲ Use emotions positively as a starting point from which to adapt.

We will illustrate the effects of emotions on your job performance and on your ability to deal with complex tasks, as well as on interpersonal relations and your management skills. This will lead to a step-by-step approach to recognizing potential symptoms and coping with the emotional and physical demands of international work.

The challenges of international work

Managers on longer-term international assignments face enormous challenges:

▲ A different job, a different country, a different house – dealing with the practicalities of settling down
▲ Not understanding the rules for the easiest practical tasks
▲ Coping with isolation
▲ Coping with the stress of the family settling in

▲ Being irritated when things don't run smoothly
▲ Not being able to work to a normal time schedule as things don't happen as planned
▲ Not understanding what really drives their local counterparts
▲ Not understanding the political undercurrents in the organization
▲ Dealing with the fact that the job is not really what they thought it was
▲ Finding other expatriates rather boring
▲ Not knowing what they can do in terms of social activities, etc.

This list is not exhaustive – but it may well make you *feel* exhausted. As one executive working in Sudan remarked:

> *"After five months, I still feel that getting used to all the differences takes all my energy."*

The first stage of emotional adaptation to any international assignment is therefore to anticipate early on the challenges you are likely to face. Secondly, envisage yourself and your emotional reactions, and finally, learn techniques that will help you deal with these situations successfully.

It is not just managers who go abroad on long assignments who are prone to stress. The demands of short-term international work and of working internationally from a home base with visits abroad are different but equally strenuous – always being on tight time schedules, frequent plane trips with many unscheduled delays, little time to understand the mentality of different nationalities, discovering how to be effective in a multicultural team, learning to be part of a virtual team and so on.

'Travel may not only broaden the mind, it may also unhinge it,' claimed an article in the *Sunday Times* (13 July 1997) investigating the effect of business travel on top executives. The results of an extensive study looking at 10,000 staff at the World Bank showed some alarming results: they suggested that frequent flying forces up to 10 percent of executives into therapy or on to medication. The Washington-based World Bank sends its staff on 18,000 missions each year, mostly to Asia, Africa and Latin America. One in ten sought prescription drugs or counseling after their return and the amount of sleep needed increased sharply with the number of trips. Each trip seems to bring a massive increase in stress and workload, which in extreme cases can result in a range of psychiatric problems, including depression and attention disorders.

The study also suggested that specific psychiatric symptoms are related to the direction of the flight. Eastbound travelers (for whom the day becomes shorter) seem more likely to suffer from signs of mania. Westbound travelers (for whom the day becomes longer) are more prone to depression. Simply crossing time zones can take its toll, an area that managers and organizations tend to neglect.

Mixed feelings

As the culture shock triangle illustrates, when we are adapting to international work our emotions range from happiness and euphoria to potential anxiety and depression. Sometimes we experience a mixture of different feelings at the same time. When we are undergoing massive changes, this mixture can be exacerbated and we feel as if we are 'slaves to our emotions'. Irritability and mood swings are normal and we seem more vulnerable to external influences than we are in our home country.

There are various reasons for experiencing unpleasant emotions. We need a great deal of energy to make the effort to adapt, which is a general strain. We feel a sense of loss and deprivation if we are not with our friends and family. We may well be confused about our role and expectations. As a consequence, we feel anxious and helpless. In extreme cases, this can result in our feeling unable to cope with the new job, the new organization or the new country.

If you are a senior manager in a high-profile position, being confused or helpless is the last thing you can admit to, either to yourself or to others. But ignoring negative emotions is the least effective thing you can do. Experiencing the emotional side of culture shock is completely normal, but it is nevertheless important to be aware when things are getting out of hand.

Effects on job performance

The symptoms of culture shock that you are experiencing can obviously affect your work, therefore it is important to be aware of the kind of situation that can arise where a symptom can become a serious problem.

Anxiety

In unfamiliar situations, we often feel anxious. We have no idea what is going to happen, we don't know how we will react and we don't know whether we will be able to cope. In international work, this is a classic scenario. While we can predict the reactions of our business counterparts in our own country fairly well and know what to do in most situations, we have no automatic responses in international encounters. It is therefore normal to feel slightly anxious and to worry. Just how much we worry depends on our personality, our self-confidence and our previous experience. Moreover, some people thrive on unpredictable situations, whereas others immediately become anxious and try to withdraw.

The degree of anxiety depends on whether we feel able to cope. If we have a great deal of self-confidence and a belief in our own abilities to deal with difficult situations, we will feel less anxious and not worry too much. If unfamiliar situations are seen as threatening because we have little confidence in our own abilities, we will be highly anxious.

A certain amount of anxiety or adrenalin can be positive – it increases our energy and alertness. But there is a point where the positive effect is reversed and increased anxiety becomes a problem. This is when anxiety is at a level that affects job performance.

Anxiety interrupts effective work patterns. If we are continually worrying about whether we are doing the right thing, we will be spending too much time on irrelevant aspects of the task. We may worry about the format and layout of a report for two hours but only spend 30 minutes thinking about its content! More importantly, when we are anxious, we lose a rational perspective. Whereas under normal circumstances we try to generate several alternatives for solving a problem and use rational criteria to select the best one, this objective and detached approach is simply not possible in a state of high anxiety; instead we jump from one solution to the next, beginning one task after another without completing anything. We cannot concentrate for any length of time.

This haphazard approach does not improve our decision making. We either delay decisions because we can't come to a rational conclusion or we take unnecessary risks. We adopt an emergency and *ad hoc* solution rather than a step-by-step approach. Because our working style is ineffective, we can run into enormous time management problems, thereby exacerbating our feelings of anxiety.

It is easy to see how this approach can lead to a vicious circle of feeling we can't handle the situation, which therefore leads to an ineffective approach and coming up with a bad solution, which in turn reinforces our original feeling of not being up to the task.

Another effect of anxiety is a general lack of planning. Instead of being proactive – working out a step-by-step approach and preempting potential problems – we become reactive. Anxiety can also have an effect on our interpersonal relationships. We will probably be more irritable and may show our emotions at inappropriate times. Alternatively, we may withdraw and try to give the impression to our colleagues that nothing is wrong.

If we are highly anxious and worrying all the time, we can't manage other people effectively. We are not able to think about how our foreign counterparts are best motivated or how we should deal with a boss from a different culture. Even if we don't show our anxiety in our verbal behavior, there can be non-verbal cues: we may appear stressed, fidgety and erratic.

Obsession

When managers feel out of control, they want to exert even more control than usual. This may show in an extreme focus on detail and minutiae. If we aren't in control of the big things, we start to become obsessed with the small things, like whether the pencils on our desk are all the same way up.

International managers often don't take enough time to think about the most effective way of doing their jobs in a new operation. Along with this, they feel pressure to make an impact as soon as possible. If this is mixed with high anxiety, it can result in a preoccupation with details – an obsession with day-to-day accounts as opposed to looking at strategy and people management; or an obsession with a particular project that is only a small part of the overall operation. Small matters take over.

Socially, managers who become obsessive show a general unease. If they are in a situation that they can't control, they are unable to cope. They shut down and become 'closed', which restricts their ability to learn new things. They may even show signs of paranoia. For example, foreign colleagues are seen as obstructive and are blamed for everything that is wrong. There is often an exaggerated fear of being taken advantage of, particularly in business negotiations. The results are a negative view of others and, ultimately, isolation.

Anxiety and obsession are related to a loss of confidence. This is even more evident in the case of depression.

Depression

If we feel anxious, we have doubts about whether we can cope and are apprehensive, but we haven't given up yet. If we feel depressed, we are already resigned to our fate – we feel we can't cope any more and our self-confidence is at rock bottom. Psychologists use the term 'learned helplessness' (Seligman, 1975) for when we believe that nothing we do has an effect and we therefore feel utterly helpless. We end up with a negative view of ourselves, the world and the future (Beck, 1967).

This is a serious condition. It has an extremely negative effect on our energy levels – there may be days when our concentration is low, we feel we can't do anything and we aren't even interested in trying.

Depression also affects our creativity and problem-solving ability. We are very tunnel visioned, everything is seen as black and white and some potential strategies are not even considered. Existing knowledge is often not used because we cannot retrieve the information from our memory. The simplest task becomes too much effort: our body shuts down and we don't always do what we need to survive, such as eating and sleeping.

When we are depressed, we become socially withdrawn and isolated. If we don't feel confident, we don't want to interact with anyone else. As a consequence, we don't build essential relationships with other people, professionally or personally, and we wallow in self-pity.

Anxiety, obsession and depression can lead to a serious deficit in performance. Moreover, managers who experience these symptoms for a long time isolate themselves from the local population and often drink too much alcohol; a classic problem in expatriate circles. It is therefore essential to see these symptoms as stress reactions and to try to reduce the stress (see the coping strategies at the end of this chapter).

Type A

There is one particular pattern of characteristics, called Type A, that is common to managers who are potentially at risk in an international arena. It was initially identified as a risk personality for coronary disease, although this assumption has been challenged.

Type A could be seen as 'the malaise of the modern manager'. Its characteristics are a high drive for achievement, impatience, haste, restlessness, being under time pressure, extreme competitiveness and aggressiveness.

Many people will recognize these symptoms. Type A managers are usually highly task oriented. They try to achieve the impossible in a short space of time. However, they lack a people orientation and may not focus on the environment in which they are working. They often don't take time to analyze the situation or listen to others, but instead forge ahead impulsively with their own ideas. As a consequence, they are probably less likely to think about developing a culturally effective style. They believe that their own style works best and that others will come round to it!

Type A behavior was identified by two cardiologists, Friedman and Rosenman, who defined it as a 'characteristic action-emotion complex which is exhibited by those individuals who are engaged in a relatively *chronic struggle* to obtain an unlimited number of *poorly defined* things from their environment in the *shortest* period of time, and, if necessary, against the opposing effects of other things or persons in the same environment' (Friedman and Rosenman, 1969; italics in original). We can transfer this definition directly to the context of international work. The struggle to adapt can become chronic and certainly the goals are initially poorly defined. There is always pressure from headquarters to produce results in a short time no matter what it takes.

Taking it to an extreme, we can easily imagine a driven, restless and highly competitive manager who would rather act like a bulldozer and impose their style on those around them than try to understand what is going on and adapt to the environment. If aggression, speed and competitiveness characterize the Type A manager, the opposite, Type B, tends to adapt rather than struggle aggressively against the environment.

Three main characteristics of Type A

Speed and impatience
Type A managers are always impatient. They do everything fast: they eat quickly, they talk rapidly, they hurry other people along and finish their sentences for them, they are often short-tempered and they become irritated easily.

Putting a Type A person into an Asian business environment can cause problems. Showing a temper, not listening and finishing other people's sentences are not seen as dignified behavior. Type A managers will lose face and will not obtain the social recognition they need to establish good business relationships.

Job involvement
Type A managers are often highly dedicated to their jobs and are driven to succeed in their careers. They are committed and work overtime to meet deadlines. However, they may become over-

ambitious and set goals higher than those set for them by the organization. The result is excessive job involvement and a lack of balance
between professional and private life.

Hard-driving and competitive nature

Type A managers are highly competitive. They focus on individual
competition as opposed to building a team. But this is not valued in
all societies. Harmony and the success of the group are more important in collectivistic societies (such as Asia) than in individualistic
societies (such as the USA or western Europe).

Are you a Type A manager?

Check Table 1 to identify any warning signs.

Table 1 Warning signs of Type A behavior

Impatience and restlessness
Extreme competitiveness
Aggressiveness and hostility
Hyper-alertness
Fast speech
Tenseness in body and face
Being under huge time pressure
Wanting to dominate
Lack of self-control
High conscientiousness and job commitment
The desire for control
Fast thinking and fast acting
Self-centered and easily angered
Poor listening

In one sense, it is good to have Type A managers in an organization. They are drivers and high achievers and they get the job done. But they can irritate and upset everyone around them. Type A managers lack interpersonal sensitivity and this is, of course, an essential skill in an international context. They simply barge on towards their goals and don't think about the casualties they leave behind. Instead of looking at how they can achieve the task together with other people, and listening and tuning into their environment, they try to control it. They react adversely to external constraints that seem to threaten their sense of control; this is exactly what happens in international work. This 'control freak' also exhibits a range of negative emotions, such as anger and hostility – a highly potent combination for creating chaos in international business.

An international manager whom I assessed for an assignment in South East Asia serves as a good illustration. This British manager had been working abroad in various parts of the world for a number of years and was highly experienced internationally. However, he showed several personality characteristics that indicated a Type A approach to management and were therefore risk areas for the assignment in South East Asia:

▲ He was highly assertive and dominant in orientation. This gave him the advantage that he knew what he wanted and had strong opinions, but he could also come across as pushy, insensitive and unable to listen to others. Particularly in relation to the non-aggressive business culture in South East Asia, this was an area to address. Although he had a good understanding of cross-cultural differences, there was some question as to whether he would give other people the time to express their opinion.

▲ Combined with his strong desire for dominance was a tendency to be straightforward and very direct in his interaction style – he lacked diplomacy, another risk factor in an Asian business setting.

▲ He showed a high vulnerability to stress and I advised him to monitor his stress level.

▲ Most importantly, he showed a Type A pattern of impatience, high job involvement and strong competitive drive. A more relaxed and analytical approach was required.

You might ask whether it is possible to change this type of behavior. Luckily, there is some evidence that Type A behavior *can* be changed, without necessarily destroying the positive effects of high achievement and drive.

Stress checklist

Most of us have felt stressed at some point in our life, but we still find it difficult to define exactly what stress is. Some psychologists go as far as saying 'stress is in the eye of the beholder' and, in a way, this is quite an accurate description. Whereas some managers feel stressed when they discover that their favorite suit is at the drycleaners, others don't seem to bat an eyelid when their company's shares take a nose dive.

Is it entirely their subjective view of a situation that makes one person feel stressed and leaves another unperturbed? Many experts would support this contention. Richard Lazarus (1966), a well-known expert in the area, explains stress on the basis of cognition or perception. In an unfamiliar situation, we try to find out whether the situation is positive or potentially threatening. We immediately evaluate our resources. If this evaluation turns out to be positive, i.e. we believe we have the resources to cope, we relax and don't feel stressed. However, if we consider our own resources to be insufficient, we feel stressed, anxious, tense and so on. In fact, you may actually have the necessary resources but if you evaluate them negatively (e.g. because of a lack of self-confidence), you will feel stressed.

The most frequent symptoms of stress are listed in Table 2.

Table 2 Symptoms of stress

Feeling tense
Feeling upset
Feeling helpless
Moodiness and irritability
Worrying
Concentration problems
Lack of performance at work
Aggressive and angry outbursts
Loss of confidence
Restlessness and inability to settle down to work
Inability to relate to others
Feelings of isolation
Weight loss
Sleeping problems (difficulties in falling asleep or waking up)
Eating problems (loss of appetite or increased appetite)
Increased alcohol intake
Inability to relax
Fear of the worst happening

What are your personal stress indicators?

Different people's stress symptoms vary enormously: some eat more, others eat less, some don't sleep, others sleep more, some get irritable and moody, some drink more, etc.

But when does 'more or less' of anything indicate stress? There are a few pointers you should look out for when the pressure mounts:

▲ Has your eating, sleeping or working pattern changed significantly?
▲ Do you exhibit behavior/symptoms that interfere with your enjoyment of life or your work?
▲ If you can identify any specific symptoms, how long have they been present and have you tried to do something about them?
▲ If you have experienced stress symptoms for an extended period,

despite efforts to reduce them, you should consider seeking professional help, either from your doctor or a therapist.

Effective strategies for coping with stress

There are innumerable articles and books on how to cope with stress and this section doesn't attempt to provide a summary of every possible stress technique. Obviously, a good diet, looking after your health, a balanced lifestyle, sport, relaxation, homeopathy and alternative medicine can all be effective in a stress-reduction program. However, we will focus here on stress in relation to the challenges of international work and consider action that can be taken through active problem solving.

Three lessons in problem solving

People have different ways of dealing with negative emotions or stress. Some try to talk to a confidant, some become more disciplined, and others take the fatalistic attitude that they will get out of the situation somehow and so they don't need to do anything about it. Everyone has ways of coping with depressive phases and has their own idiosyncratic remedies. Practical advice given for dealing with culture shock in general is useful in handling stress, but it is not sufficient. It is more effective to supplement it with some basic lessons on problem solving.

There are three main strategies for tackling stress that we will describe in detail: anticipation, emotion-focused coping and problem-focused coping (Lazarus and Folkman, 1984).

Anticipation

You have already won half the battle if you are aware of the potential problems you are facing and have anticipated the negative emotions. A review of your own reactions in difficult situations and an evaluation of your emotional vulnerability will give you an idea of how hard the culture shock may hit. Seeing stress and culture shock as 'normal'

also puts things into perspective. This can create a much more positive, 'can do' attitude.

Emotion-focused coping

As in any crisis, we have to do two things: keep our emotions under
control and do something about the problem. The first is sometimes
called 'emotion-focused coping', the second 'problem-focused
coping'.

Emotion-focused coping isn't a sign of weakness. It often involves
the necessary activity of calming down and stilling your nerves before
going into action.

Negative emotions are often precipitated by unrealistic assumptions or unconstructive attitudes. Examples include:

▲ "This is the biggest mistake I have ever made."
▲ "I hate the food, the flat, the country and the people."
▲ "Nothing here is as good."
▲ "People don't understand me."
▲ "Things will never change."
▲ "I have failed to adapt and I will be a total failure throughout."
▲ "Catastrophe is just around the corner."

If you want to change negative emotions, you have to identify, challenge and change the negative assumptions that caused them. Replacing unrealistic assumptions with a more realistic attitude leads to
more positive emotions.

The effect that our thinking has on our emotions is illustrated in
Figure 4.

Not everyone suffers from unrealistic or negative assumptions.
But if you can identify them, it is worth challenging them and seeing
whether replacing them with more realistic assumptions will have an
effect on your emotional well-being.

Unrealistic assumptions not only influence how we feel but also
our problem-solving ability and our efforts to change unpleasant situations. If you believe that it is only you who has all these problems,
you may wallow in self-pity rather than actively doing something
about the situation. If, instead, you expect problems to be a normal

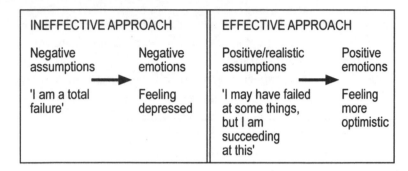

INEFFECTIVE APPROACH		EFFECTIVE APPROACH	
Negative assumptions	Negative emotions	Positive/realistic assumptions	Positive emotions
'I am a total failure'	Feeling depressed	'I may have failed at some things, but I am succeeding at this'	Feeling more optimistic

Figure 4 Effects of thinking on feeling

part of life, you will feel different and will put in more effort. A positive attitude is essential in overcoming difficult situations and work problems.

Problem-focused coping

In our study of international managers, the most frequent coping responses for coping with culture shock were the following:

▲ Perseverance and actively trying to solve the problem (used by 47 percent of managers in my survey): "Sort out what the problem is and actively do something about it."
▲ Social support from other expatriates, friends and family (used by 30 percent).
▲ A positive outlook (used by 20 percent): "Try not to take things personally, expect uncertainty, keep an open mind, laugh at frustrations."

Different coping strategies work for different people. However, one trend emerged from my findings: managers who reported short spells of culture shock used social support more frequently than those who reported long spells. It seems that social support may act as an effective buffer against the worst symptoms of culture shock. This is consistent with previous research on stress, showing that support through friends and family helps to relieve it.

Problem-focused coping and active problem solving can take different forms. Once you are in better shape emotionally, you could:

▲ Try to intensify your contact with host nationals so that you feel more involved in the local culture and learn faster about its values, attitudes and habits.

▲ Discuss your own experiences with other international managers, and use this 'mirroring' technique and the social support that goes with it to develop constructive solutions.

▲ Join local and expatriate sports clubs or pursue other hobbies that will bring you into close contact with other people.

▲ Spend more time listening and trying to understand your local colleagues. The gap between expatriate and local staff often seems insurmountable, and establishing strong contacts from the very beginning may prevent this problem or at least reduce it.

▲ Once you have identified the main source of your feelings of alienation or disorientation, you can start to tackle them in a constructive way: the beginning of all active problem solving is a thorough problem analysis.

Real-life problem solving usually follows quite distinct phases (D'Zurilla and Goldfried, 1971), as illustrated in Figure 5. Problem-solving skills can be improved if you follow a model like this.

Our general problem orientation has a significant influence on the entire problem-solving process. If you have a positive, optimistic attitude, you will reach better solutions. In contrast, if you have a 'can't do', pessimistic attitude, you won't solve problems as easily and you may not adapt to an international business culture.

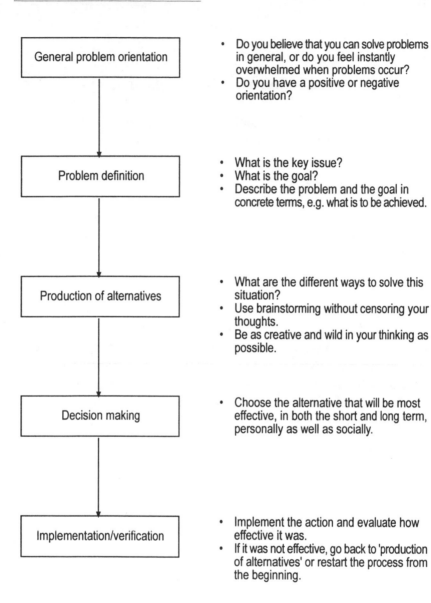

General problem orientation	• Do you believe that you can solve problems in general, or do you feel instantly overwhelmed when problems occur? • Do you have a positive or negative orientation?
Problem definition	• What is the key issue? • What is the goal? • Describe the problem and the goal in concrete terms, e.g. what is to be achieved.
Production of alternatives	• What are the different ways to solve this situation? • Use brainstorming without censoring your thoughts. • Be as creative and wild in your thinking as possible.
Decision making	• Choose the alternative that will be most effective, in both the short and long term, personally as well as socially.
Implementation/verification	• Implement the action and evaluate how effective it was. • If it was not effective, go back to 'production of alternatives' or restart the process from the beginning.

Figure 5 Problem-solving phases

Dealing with your emotions

The following strategies may help you to cope with the emotional and physical demands of international work:

▲ Check your self-perception and self-image (list positives and negatives and areas for self-development).

▲ Concentrate on the positive aspects and use your social support system effectively. Try to talk about your problems with close friends, mentors and professional contacts.

▲ Look at the way you perceive and interpret situations (are these realistic or do you suffer from unrealistic assumptions, excessive standards and negative expectations?). Get rid of the assumption that life has to be perfect.

▲ Differentiate between those situations you can control and those you can't. Try to do something about the first group and take a pragmatic approach to the second – don't worry unnecessarily about situations you can do nothing about.

▲ Watch your diet and exercise level and develop a healthy lifestyle.

3
Thinking Differently

Effective management is difficult enough in your own country: trying to understand what makes your subordinate, colleague or boss tick, finding out what management style would be effective in your organization at a particular point in time, while always being aware of the 'bottom line'. Add in the factor of culture and cross-cultural management situations easily reach new heights of complexity.

Cultural differences are particularly evident in the way people think. The following comments illustrate some of the management situations that international executives in my research experienced (Marx, 1996a):

> *"In the West, there is all the talk of empowerment which, in a way, distances the boss from the employee because there is an attitude that one gives the task to the employee and the employees can do it how they want. In the East, this idea is not really welcome because of the distancing in the relationship between boss and employee. In the East, much stronger values are based on the relationship side and one very much has to adapt to that style of management. Consequently, there is a serious question of how possible the implementation of empowerment is in the Eastern culture."*

"In France, it is difficult to understand the hierarchy and when to use first names. There is much more respect for the boss in a sort of autocratic way. In the UK, there is more consensus decision making. As a foreigner, you can get away with more but you have to be sensitive at the same time. In that way, you can use your cultural difference to an advantage."

"I was heading up the salesforce in the Hong Kong office and I had to deal with the cultural differences and the racism. The major problem was the employees would not give me any news and would not tell me what was going on. I solved this particular problem by building up individual relationships with them."

"The biggest management problem was little sensitivity to other ways of thinking. In a way, it is like being on a tightrope, one has to assimilate and renegotiate."

In this research, I asked 45 executives of various nationalities working all over the world about the main business problems they experienced. Table 3 describes the most frequently reported problems.

These cross-cultural problems illustrate some fundamental differences in business practices. For example, the extent to which relationship building is valued, the style of communication and interacting, or democratic versus autocratic styles.

Other fundamental problems were caused by the application of western management procedures to other cultures. Examples included performance-related pay in Spain and empowerment in the Far East.

In addition, there is the fact that international positions often represent promotions and sometimes more training is needed in general management, independent of the cross-cultural angle.

Table 3 Problems most frequently reported by international managers

Cross-cultural problems

Switching from a more bureaucratic approach to a relationship-building
approach (as in China)

Differences in interaction style

Getting used to more autocratic procedures and a more hierarchical
system (as in France or the UAE)

Being in a less straightforward and more political organizational
environment (as in France)

Dealing with racist attitudes

Coping with a paternalistic attitude (as in Italy)

General management problems

Dealing with high staff turnover and lack of loyalty (as in Singapore)

Little team orientation

Problems with boss

Unequal pay between expatriates and local managers

Dealing with conflicts

Dealing with corruption

Understanding other people

A German HR manager had been asked to organize the visit of a
group of Indonesian businessmen who were coming to Germany for
a professional exchange. This was a last-minute request by her organization and therefore she had little time to prepare.

As a consequence, she was confronted with several problems:

▲ The Indonesian businessmen did not keep to any agendas or
time schedules. The German organization provided an agenda of
different activities during the visit, but none of the Indonesian
managers complied with it.

▲ In a group discussion, the Indonesian managers were asked to
share their opinions on various management issues and to give a

critical analysis of business situations. However, the German coordinator was unable to get them to participate.

▲ The Germans were upset by the table manners of their Indonesian colleagues. Indonesians use forks and spoons and are not used to eating with knives.

This experience taught the German HR manager several lessons:

▲ Time schedules did not make sense to the Indonesians. The Germans should have been aware of this and organized the visit differently.
▲ It is impolite in the Indonesian culture to ask for direct feedback and particularly to ask for expressions of criticism. It is inconsistent with the concept of harmony which is valued in the Indonesian culture.
▲ As the Germans were hosting this particular event, they should have been more sensitive to the eating customs of Indonesians and provided their guests with the cutlery they normally used.

Culture

The biggest challenge in international management is understanding other people's culture, which manifests itself in different ways. We use the word culture all the time without considering the exact definition, but in this context, we can define culture as 'the way things are done'. Obviously, this can express itself in various forms.

Hofstede (1994), a well-known author in this area, suggested that we should look at cultural manifestations from an outer layer to an inner layer (see Figure 6).

Symbols

On the outer layer of culture we find symbols, which could include gestures, dress code, class symbols, etc. Even within one culture, there are many symbols characterizing different classes (we could take bourgeois dressing in France or Wasps in the USA).

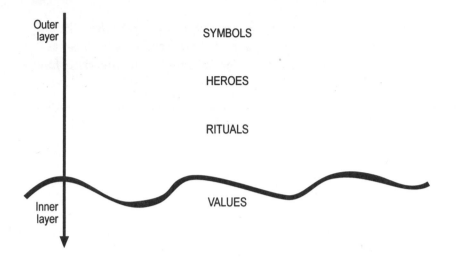

Figure 6 Hofstede's manifestations of culture

You will find cultural differences in practically all everyday activities, including:

▲ Greeting

"In many Asian societies, the first question in greeting a new-comer is 'How is your family?' – something that seems strange to a northern European. "

▲ The art of small talk or conversation
▲ Clothes and dress code

A video on cross-cultural business starts with members of a multi-national team arriving for a meeting. The team coordinator, a British national, is already present when the German contingent arrives. "Did the airline lose your suitcase?" the British national enquired when spotting the Germans wearing blazers rather than full suits – not realizing that this was their normal business attire.

▲ Table manners
▲ Meal times and type of food

"The French practice of business lunches is prevalent. Hours are spent each day lunching with business contacts. Business, however, is only discussed for a short time; never before dessert."

▲ Office hours and shopping hours
▲ Entertaining
▲ Schooling
▲ Health and preventive medicine
▲ Religious practices.

Heroes

In the next layer of culture we find heroes. These are real or imaginary figures of special importance within a given culture, such as:

▲ John F Kennedy in the USA
▲ Jean-Paul Sartre in France
▲ Winston Churchill in the UK.

Rituals

Next are rituals, ceremonies marking special occasions, such as funeral rites, or tea ceremonies in Japan.

"In Chinese society, a newborn baby is celebrated at the one-month party. Extended family, friends and business contacts are invited to celebrate the baby's arrival with an elaborate Chinese banquet in a restaurant. This is also the first time when the baby's hair is cut."

"The Balinese Temple Festivals, which go on all night with music, and people dancing in a trance, are one of the most extraordinary religious festivals."

> *"You can see the rituals of Black Magic in Brazil – with special candles and flowers on Rio's beaches at night."*

Rituals give the newcomer some idea of the importance of a particular event within the society or the event's significance in the eyes of the group for which the ritual takes place. However, often many questions remain unanswered.

> *"During the 'Hungry Ghost' Festival in the eighth month of the Chinese Calendar, we observed a ritual with two Chinese falling into a trance and assuming the roles of two deities (black and white); the two deities, with the accompanying group of 'fellow believers' subsequently moved from the City center to a cemetery for a further ritual."*

> *"The Carnival in Cologne is a serious affair of enjoyment. For three days, Germans go mad and are literally encouraged to be 'fools'. They party solidly for three days, with masquerades of varying degrees, and the rule is that you can do what you want during these three days. Serious businessmen are found dancing on tables, and women cut men's ties off."*

Values

Rituals have history, particular origins and a specific context that gives them meaning. They stand for much more than meets the eye. To comprehend what symbols, heroes and rituals really mean, one needs to understand the values behind them. In contrast to symbols and rituals that are overt or explicit, values are covert or implicit – they are not directly observable and require time and effort to comprehend. However, they form the basis of all cultural differences.

Values are 'standards or principles considered valuable or important in life' (*Oxford Paperback Dictionary*). They are deep-rooted attitudes that have a significant influence on people's behavior. They express what people really believe in, their attitudes towards the most important topics in life (their part in society, attitudes towards relationships, time and nature etc.). Values will determine how we feel, think and behave and reflect our cultural background. Values are influenced by the history of a group or nation. They are learned as part of socialization: what a child can and cannot do, what behavior towards authority should be like, what is right and wrong, good and bad, beautiful and ugly.

The following comments illustrate cultural values that have a direct effect on working behavior:

> "*Germany and France have different attitudes in the work-place. Germany has a lack of flexibility and in France people are highly individualistic. For example, if the* Vorstand *(board) in Germany asks a senior manager to do something which is outside his prescribed responsibility, he may simply decline on that basis.*"

> "*As a Brit in France, I had to be more autocratic and tough. You can't go for consensus decision making because otherwise they think you are a 'softy'.*"

Most of the time, we are quite unaware or cannot verbalize what our values are because they are very complex, were acquired a long time ago and are often subconscious. Ask yourself what your most important values are and you will see how difficult it is.

Yet it is the understanding of different values that will bring us closest to cross-cultural effectiveness. In order to understand how other people think, it is necessary to understand their value system, but to understand others, we need to be aware of and understand our own value system.

A practical exercise may help with understanding values in business.

Improving your cross-cultural management skills

Consider how you would solve the situation described below. I will offer some concrete suggestions later in the chapter.

You are part of a business development group in your organization. Your team's task is to win a contract for a new project with the Brazilian government. You are competing for the contract with teams from the USA and Argentina.

  You have quite a lot of background information on the proposed project and on your competitors. Based on this information and your own organizational resources, you feel confident that you will win the contract.

  Your proposal is time and cost effective and your presentation is based on convincing numbers and a rational argument. However, you eventually lose the project to the Argentinian team.

  Make some notes in relation to the following issues:

▲ Why do you think the Argentinian team obtained the contract? List several possible reasons.
▲ How could your strategy for doing business in Brazil be improved?

Three dimensions of culture

Most of today's work on cultural dimensions is based on Geert Hofstede's research in this area, which was followed up and expanded by Fons Trompenaars. Culture in this context is defined as mental programs or, as Hofstede suggested, a 'software of the mind' – 'a collective programming of the mind that distinguishes the members of one group or category of people from another' (1994, p5). The main assumption is that people from different cultures all face the same basic problems (such as the relationship to authority or the concept of self). However, the way people solve these problems differs from culture to culture.

In an attempt to identify these different problem-solving techniques, both Hofstede and Trompenaars conducted extensive
research and found evidence of different cultural dimensions.
Depending on which of the two systems one favors, there are either
four or seven cultural dimensions. These influence the way we work
and can therefore explain clashes in international business. However,
some of the dimensions also seem to overlap and are not completely
independent.

I was curious to discover whether there are some essential underlying dimensions in both models that could explain cross-cultural differences in a more succinct way. If so, this would reduce the number
of dimensions and make our life in international business more simple. To pursue this, instead of deciding which theory is substantiated
by better data, I attempted to define the three basic questions that a
manager should ask in every international business situation, based on
my practical work in coaching international managers.

The following three questions seem to be essential:

▲ Is the focus primarily on the task at hand or on people?
▲ Are frameworks more important than flexibility?
▲ What is the dominant communication and presentation style?

These questions lead to a pragmatic classification of cultural differences, as outlined in Figure 7.

The three key areas cover the main misunderstandings in cross-
cultural management:

▲ Where is the focus and how fast can I do the task? How much
  effort should I put into building relationships?
▲ How explicit and detailed does my framework have to be? Can I
  rely on schedules that my business partner gives me?
▲ Should I follow a rational, emotion-free presentation style or
  should I try to liven it up with some humor and emotion? Can I
  talk about critical issues or do I have to gloss over these and stay
  positive at all times? Should I be formal or informal?

It may sound paradoxical to suggest that focusing on these areas will
also help you to overcome a one-sided and stereotypical view of

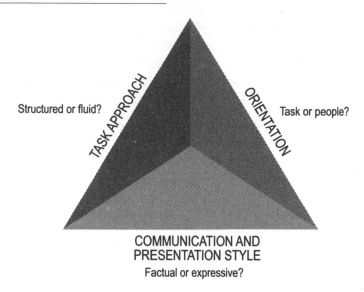

Figure 7 The three main dimensions in cross-cultural management

culture, but this illustrates one of the most important features of cross-cultural effectiveness, namely the use of frameworks that allow for individual exceptions. In other words, we need a framework to understand international business situations, without becoming prescriptive about it. For example, it is not because all Germans are bureaucratic that I should send an agenda, but rather because many German companies have a very structured work approach and it is therefore useful to check whether I should send an agenda or not. What is essential is not a prescriptive action, but the ability to think of alternative ways of doing things.

I will refer to both Hofstede's and Trompenaars' work in describing these key areas.

Orientation

Cultures differ in their orientation to the task or to relationships/ people. Western cultures are generally more task oriented (particularly in northern Europe and the USA) compared to Asia or South America. A US manager wants to whizz into the company, sort things out, get out and go to the next job. Hong Kong or Singaporean managers will first try to establish good relationships before looking at the deal. Asian executives look at how the system works and see individuals as part of a system. In contrast, their northern European and US counterparts will try to break the venture down into parts, compartmentalize it and get the task done before moving on to the next one.

This dimension can be seen as a reflection of individualism versus collectivism and of a focus on specifics versus a focus on the context.

Individualism versus collectivism

Are our actions primarily influenced by our own urges, goals and motivation or by those of the group to which we belong? In individualist societies (such as North America and northern Europe) the focus is on the self, as reflected in the idea of self-actualization (at the top of Maslow's hierarchy of needs). In contrast, in collectivist societies (for example China and some of the former communist countries) the prime motivation is towards the common objectives of the group.

We could say that this dimension depends on our definition of self. Individuals from collectivist cultures make more reference to the group as part of their self-definition, whereas individuals from individualist cultures make reference to self-attributes ("I am part of the X family" as opposed to "I am good at languages").

For example, when I worked at the National University of Singapore, we asked a group of Singaporean students to fill in a self-concept test which consisted of 20 statements starting with "I am..." Compared to US students, Singaporeans (although often fairly westernized) were much more likely to see themselves as part of the group or the family; they were more collectivist than individually oriented.

*Table 4 Examples of cultures on opposite poles –
individualism versus collectivism*

Individualism	Collectivism
USA	South Korea
UK	Thailand
	Singapore

As Trompenaars and Hampden-Turner (1998) have illustrated, this dimension influences negotiations, decision making and motivation:

▲ *Negotiations.* Negotiations in collectivist cultures are often attended by a group of people, as opposed to a sole representative in individualist cultures. This has the implication that unaccompanied people may be seen as lacking status in collectivist societies.
▲ *Decision making.* Collectivist decision making takes longer, as the focus is on consensus or checking back with headquarters. The advantage is that decisions are well thought through and implementation can usually proceed quite smoothly.
▲ *Motivation.* In individualist societies, performance-related pay is effective. In collectivist societies, individual performance-related pay may not make much sense and may be ineffective, as many western organizations have experienced when trying to apply their procedures in a non-western culture.

Specifics versus context

Individualist cultures have a tendency to compartmentalize and to concentrate on specific tasks. Collectivist cultures are more context oriented and see most tasks as interrelated.

Different areas of life are connected. For example, in context-oriented cultures, business negotiations start with building relationships and proceed from the periphery to the core objective of the meeting. Specific-oriented cultures concentrate on the core business objectives

first and may later engage in peripheral or social activities, although
these are not regarded as absolutely necessary.

Context-oriented cultures are characterized by task orientation
through people orientation. It follows that in context-oriented cultures,
you need more time to establish business relationships. You cannot
carry out negotiations on the basis of rational arguments or the logic of
product superiority. In fact, this is what may have gone wrong in the
Brazilian business situation described in the case example: an exclusive
presentation of rational arguments (a specific focus) without considering more extensive aspects of the business and negotiations.

*An example of a highly task-oriented British manager (coming
from a specific culture) going to work in Thailand (a more
context-oriented culture) may illustrate this dimension. The
psychological assessment established certain risk areas concerning the British manager's personality profile and the culture in
which he was going to work. The candidate had an extremely
straightforward and direct interaction approach. He was also very
assertive and dominant. Both characteristics are risk factors in the
Thai business environment where harmony and diplomatic behavior are valued.*

*The candidate was highly task driven and competitive. He was
also very pragmatic and bottom-line oriented. Whereas these are
very positive within a western business context, they tend to be
counter-productive in Asia. In order to set up a company in Thailand and develop business, this manager needed to take a more
strategic and long-term approach. He also had to work on his ability to develop business relationships, as he was an introvert and
therefore not automatically inclined to establish the social
networks that are important for business in Thailand. In general,
going from a specific to a context orientation was one of the main
coaching areas for this candidate.*

*Table 5 Examples of cultures on opposite poles –
          specific versus context*

Specific culture	Context-oriented culture
USA	China
UK	Indonesia
Germany	Singapore
	Thailand

Task approach – structured versus fluid

Our approach to a task may be more structured or more fluid, depending on the influence of our cultural background. We may need to work to a framework, or we may be able to be more flexible. This dimension may also be considered in terms of how far we are able to tolerate ambiguity, and how we think about time.

Tolerance of ambiguity

People from different cultures react very differently in ambiguous situations. At one extreme, the German culture is characterized by intolerance of ambiguity. This is one of the reasons that Germans are highly structured, organized, work with clear agendas and do not like unpredictability. They are very time conscious, concrete in their planning and work to a step-by-step approach. They are well prepared when they come to meetings and follow exactly the priorities of the agenda.

At the other extreme is Brazil, where planning is not so important and what is paramount is that the objective is achieved. Therefore, Brazilian business partners go much more with the flow, have a fairly fluid approach, are not too bothered with agendas and can change direction quite easily.

The tolerance of ambiguity in a particular culture determines whether frameworks and structures are put in place and adhered to strictly, and possibly also how much time is spent working on the bureaucracy of business, since cultures with a high tolerance of ambiguity are almost by definition more fluid and less structured. It is easy to imagine the potential difficulties when representatives of the extreme poles meet in business negotiations – the Germans may despair of the unstructured approach of the Brazilians and the Brazilians may find the Germans rigid and bureaucratic.

But let us not forget that there may be significant individual differences within a particular culture. Individuals differ in the extent to which they prefer complexity and ambiguity as opposed to certainty. It is often managers who prefer ambiguity who do particularly well in international settings, as these are by definition ambiguous and complex. By contrast, managers who want an excessive amount of certainty and rigid frameworks will not adapt well to this unpredictability.

Table 6 Examples of cultures on opposite poles –
tolerance of ambiguity

Low	High
Germany	Brazil
	India

Time concept

The way we think about time has a strong influence on how we organize our activities with others. Following Trompenaars and Hampden-Turner's (1998) categorization, cultures see time as either sequential (a series of passing events) or synchronic (where past, present and future are interrelated).

Western cultures often have a sequential time concept: we see the way from A to B as a straight line and therefore plan everything to tight and efficient time schedules. This is stringent forward planning or a 'time is money' attitude. However, in synchronic societies, the emphasis is on doing several activities at the same time and this is still considered normal practice. For example, a manager may be on the phone, having a conversation with someone else in the room and be taking notes, all at the same time. In Brazil, it is perfectly acceptable to answer your mobile phone in a business meeting.

Hall and Hall (1990, p14) explain sequential thinking as follows:

It is an artifact of the industrial revolution in England; factory life required the labor force to be on hand and in place at an appointed hour. In spite of the fact that it is learned, monochronic (i.e. sequential) time now appears to be natural and logical because the great majority of Americans grew up in monochronic time systems with whistles and bells counting off the hours.

In sequential societies, people plan everything, they work to time schedules and there is a great focus on punctuality. In synchronic cultures, there is less focus on being on time. The basic idea is to agree the general objectives of the project and then find a way to reach them. Flexibility is more valued than schedules.

When we are working across cultures, it is important to ascertain the significance of the past and of traditions. This is a common failure of western management consultants. International business projects may fail because of a disregard for counterparts' cultural background and approach to work. Synchronic cultures carry their past through to the present and to the future. They will refuse to consider change unless they can be convinced that their heritage is safe. Therefore, western consultants have to adapt their approach to this framework and show that traditions are not threatened by new ways of working or by technology.

The American sequential approach is seen by synchronic cultures as aggressive and impatient. Sequential planning also works less well in fast-changing, turbulent environments, such as those experienced in the 1990s.

In my own experience, adapting to different time schedules and frameworks is extremely difficult. Being German, I was trained to take a very stringent approach to any task, with all details organized and all eventualities incorporated. This perfectionist approach makes you very vulnerable in working environments that have different rules. I took a long time to relax. Although in some ways I am probably still more structured than flexible, I have developed quite an effective style: my planning is much more long term, oriented towards larger goals, which leaves more flexibility in dealing with details. I schedule in more obstacles and this also allows me to change plans. Most importantly, I do not run a project sequentially but take a synchronic approach and do several things at once, which allows me to progress with a particular project when the time is right. This gives me flexibility but also allows sufficient planning.

Table 7 Examples of cultures on opposite poles –
*   time concept*

Sequential	**Synchronic**
USA	Brazil
Germany	Southern Europe

Communication and presentation style

Whereas Italian and French managers show their emotions, Chinese managers prize composed and cool behavior. Some cultures are formal and put a high value on titles, seniority and hierarchies, whereas others take a much more informal, democratic approach and work on the basis of meritocracy, independent of the age or origin of the person.

Factual versus expressive style

In some cultures, the expression of emotions (in tone of voice or gesture) is fully encouraged, whereas in others emotional expression is unacceptable and is seen as a sign of weakness or loss of control. Emotional expression is part of business life in Latin countries, whereas

Asian countries, such as Japan or China, would find this intolerable and see it as a loss of 'face' and therefore a loss of respect. Trompenaars and Hampden-Turner (1998) define this contrast in viewpoints as being the difference between neutral and affective cultures.

During my work in Singapore, staff meetings were an absolutely classic example of cross-cultural communication. Singaporeans typically behaved in a rational and unemotional way when expressing their opinions in group meetings. They wanted to find a harmonious solution and therefore focused on consensus decision making. Ultimately, they did not want to lose face. Western expatriates, in contrast, debated ferociously, showing anger, frustration and enthusiasm, and generally did not care whether their opinions were extreme and against the majority. Interestingly, most of these situations worked out OK because everybody recognized and accepted the others' style and the different cultural rules – despite frustrations on both sides. The fact that we were psychologists might have helped in this respect!

There are business situations in which emotional behavior results in loss of face and respect and, ultimately, in the loss of the relationship with foreign business partners. But even if emotions can be freely expressed, there is a question about the type of emotion that is acceptable. Researchers point out cross-cultural differences in the acceptability of emotions (Harré and Parrott, 1996). For example, US culture is obsessed with positive and optimistic presentation; consequently, assertiveness, positive self-presentation and optimism are highly valued in the USA. This means that the expression of regret and self-effacing behavior are less acceptable.

*Table 8 Examples of cultures on opposite poles –
          neutral versus affective*

Neutral (factual)   **Affective (expressive)**

UK   Italy
China   Brazil
Singapore   France
Japan
Indonesia

Formal versus informal style

How is status attributed to an individual? Some cultures have a meritocratic approach and define status in terms of achievement, i.e. by
what people have done in the past; examples are educational achievements, business achievements, achievements in personal or social life.
Other cultures ascribe status by predetermined roles, by seniority or
according to age, gender or class.

The difference may result in cultures that are more formal and title
oriented (ascription) and others that are much more informal and
democratically oriented (achievement).

In an international setting, we cannot assume that status is defined
by the same standards. If an executive from an achievement-oriented
culture meets an executive from an ascription-oriented culture, the
first has to make sure that respect is given on the basis of seniority,
title, etc. In the same way, executives from an ascription-oriented
society can expect a very informal communication style from executives from more achievement-oriented societies. A good example of
these differences can be seen in the contrast between American and
Japanese executives.

Table 9 Examples of cultures on opposite poles –
  achievement versus ascription

Achievement (informal)	Ascription (formal)
USA	Indonesia
Norway	Thailand
UK	Spain
Germany	
Australia	

Cross-cultural effectiveness

The main objective of the culture shock triangle is to provide a framework to increase our cross-cultural effectiveness by enabling us to gain a deeper understanding of our colleagues' cultures. The three key areas of cultural differences provide a general framework that allows us to come up with alternative interpretations of a given situation – they do not provide a template of precise actions to be taken in particular circumstances.

Now that you have some understanding of cultural differences, it would be useful to go back to the practical exercise on page 47 and reflect on your answers. Would you change your mind about anything?

Case example

The Argentinian team may have won the contract because:

▲ They did not rely exclusively on rational argument, but spent time
  building relationships with their future partners.
▲ They understood more about the cultural sensitivities of the situation.
▲ They had a different time schedule (longer and more flexible) than
  the western team.
▲ They showed more respect for the ascription-oriented culture.
▲ They took the collectivist culture into consideration.

The aim of acquiring a cultural framework is to be able to adopt *cultural relativism* (Hofstede, 1994), the concept that admits that there is no absolute right or wrong – that no one approach is the best – and that acknowledges that a variety of approaches can be effective, depending on the particular cultural context. Being able to change methods according to the situation in which you find yourself is a key part of breaking through culture shock.

If we adopt cultural relativism, instead of assuming that A's behavior means B, we will be in a position to say that A's behavior could mean X, Y or Z, and therefore several types of reaction may be appropriate.

Being an effective international manager means that you don't apply narrow, black-and-white categories but develop different ways of looking at a situation. It also implies a strong self-knowledge, of our own culture and of our individual preferences – only if you understand yourself and the way you think can you begin to understand people from different cultures.

What happens if we don't adopt an attitude of cultural relativism? Without cross-cultural training, we have no automatic responses in an unfamiliar situation. Unfamiliarity can cause anxiety and stress. We try to reduce this anxiety and, under stress, we resort to well-proven, automatic methods that may not be effective. These responses are likely to be ethnocentric, monocultural and inappropriate.

Thinking across cultures

Review your style of approaching business situations in the three areas discussed in this chapter and train yourself to think of alternative interpretations. Only if you can meet a complex foreign environment with an equally complex range of interpretations will you be successful in international business. This method of thinking across cultures is summarized in Figure 8.

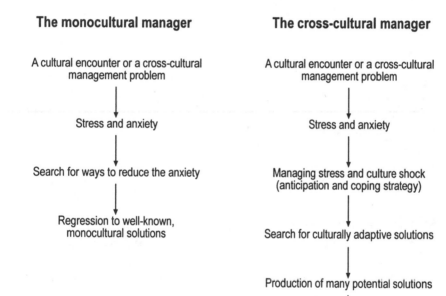

Figure 8 Thinking across cultures

4

Behaving Differently

W hat are the social skills needed in international work? How do managers adapt socially to an international role? How does their view of themselves and others change as a result of international work?

How your identity, expectations and goals will change

Most executives would be considered relatively mature individuals who have a pretty good idea of who they are and their goals in life. Our identity and goals are normally determined by our past experiences, family background, career and social context. We achieve stability through having family or close friends, through belonging to various social clubs or sports organizations and, last but not least, through being an employee of a certain company. But all this can change if we are working in another country, because the stable social and organizational set-up we take so much for granted may no longer be there.

Although our sense of identity may initially be the same (that is, we know who we are), uncertainty creeps in: we miss the familiar social context. International managers often complain about difficulties on the social side if they are on a longer-term assignment: they feel lonely and miss their friends and family, or they describe how difficult it is to build a social network. With the loss of their normal background, managers begin to doubt and question themselves. It is as if they are living in a vacuum without the signs that usually confirm their role and status; and without a predictable social context, we begin to wonder who we are.

As time goes by, international managers learn to cope with the situation. But are they the same people that they were before? It is naive to assume that a major change or exposure to a new professional or social setting will not have some kind of impact. As my research has shown, most managers report distinct changes in their personality, particularly related to their social skills (Marx, 1996a). They notice, as a consequence of their work:

▲ Greater confidence
▲ Better listening ability
▲ More tolerance and patience
▲ Greater sensitivity to other cultures
▲ Better understanding of people
▲ More assertiveness and independence
▲ Greater diplomacy
▲ A higher degree of flexibility.

A Dutch manager working in Britain described the change in her personality as follows:

> " *I* had to learn how to bite my tongue and to become more tactful. I slowed down and I'm not as vocal as I was before, for example, in taking charge of a group. I also learned to listen more. In a way, I have become quite Anglicized in that I find the more energetic discussions at home in the Netherlands a bit stressful. "

A banker working in Russia reported:

> " *I* can see how my ways of behaving and communicating have been influenced by being in Russia. I observed a similar effect with an Austrian colleague in the London bank who had come back from the US and had been very Americanized. "

Another manager commented:

> *" I feel more assertive, much more sure of myself. I am in a very demanding environment, having improved my language skills, I also find that my professional life is better. I do not see things as a problem, I see them as a challenge now. "*

Many changes are related to communication and relationship skills and successful international managers will be strong in these areas. With the acquisition of better communication and interpersonal skills, another area will change: expectations in relation to our career and life in general. In other words, our life values may alter as a consequence of international work.

This is confirmed by a British executive who worked in the USA and Africa:

> *" I always thought that I would like working internationally. I think the greatest effect it has is really on identity. "*

International executives often have very high expectations of themselves, their careers and their social life. As they start enjoying a range of different experiences, they expect a similar or even greater diversity wherever they go next, but this expectation can create difficulties when repatriating after a long-term assignment. The home setting may now be too small and unadventurous to fulfill their need for expansion and to match their new identity.

Identity is a very abstract concept, so it may be easier to think about how our interests and values change as a consequence of international work. This will ultimately depend on one fundamental decision – which lifestyle we decide to adopt.

Joining the cocktail set or going native?

This decision is characteristic of the classic expatriate. However, it applies equally to short-term international assignments, as an executive's social network will influence their expectations as well as their cross-cultural effectiveness – 'you are who you socialize with'.

Traditionally, expatriate managers clearly fell into the cocktail set category. We can read about them in short stories by Somerset Maugham or Paul Theroux. Even though there are decades separating these two writers, their descriptions of life in a foreign culture are surprisingly similar. The fundamental issues (relationship dynamics, attitudes towards life, the experience of being a 'foreigner') do not seem to have changed much.

Even today, we find classic expatriate circles in cities such as Hong Kong, Singapore or Tokyo. Many international managers in these places enjoy substantial expatriate packages as 'compensation' for not living in their home country. They have comfortable apartments provided by their company, household staff and membership of prestigious clubs. The cocktail-set manager is a club person – whether it is a sports club or a club of compatriots. The underlying motivation is always the same: finding refuge from the hustle and bustle and the foreignness of the place and retreating into our own culture, where we know that the cocktail is served with just the right amount of ice or lemon. More importantly, it is a place where we meet 'people like us'.

A senior banking executive with a long international career described the following experience:

" I had knowledge of the Far East. I was brought up in the Far East until the age of eight. I subsequently did my National Service overseas and then went to the Hong Kong and Shanghai Bank with the sole intention of going overseas and having a proper expatriate career. Hong Kong Bank at the time only recruited people who intended to work overseas. Typically, they were recruited straight from school or following National Service, and served overseas until they retired at the age of 53.

The selection at the time was pretty crude. I suspect I was selected on the basis that I had been to an English public school, and was therefore better prepared for separation from parents! In those days, overseas tours were four years without home leave. The entry qualifications at that time were not very demanding; everything went much more on personal recommendation.

At the beginning of my international career, there was some loneliness and homesickness but the bank had very strong family/social values. One of the rules of joining at the time was not to get married for the first five years. Bachelors went out from the UK and lived in a communal Mess, run on military lines, with other bachelors and formed close relationships which were often maintained throughout their careers. It was a tight social network which helped to give support. The extreme consequence of this network was having to ask the staff controller before getting married whether the person one intended to marry was 'suitable'. In the past, the bank's culture had quite a military bias to it. Thirty years ago, Hong Kong was mainly British and, therefore, not much adaptation in terms of management was required. "

Hong Kong and Shanghai Bank (now HSBC Holdings plc) is unusual in that it still has an international cadre of 370 executives. However, recruitment and retention policies are now very different from those described above. Graduates only are recruited up to the age of 27, and they may continue to work overseas until their late fifties. They must be fully mobile and be prepared to take an unusual assignment in any location. They may head up country operations or work on short-term projects. They are an elite group, with solid expatriate packages, who promote globally the HSBC Group's core values.

Large multinational companies usually have strong social establishments. In some cases, there are large company compounds where all expatriates live together (for example Shell in Sarawak).

Being part of the cocktail set allows us strict control over our environment and enables us to preserve our existing values, perspectives and perceptions. It encourages an 'us and them' attitude which can be comforting – but only for a short time. International managers often drift into this set simply because it is the natural thing to do. On arrival in a foreign place, we look for the support and comfort of compatriots – people who can give sound advice on what it is like to live there, practical information on where to shop and how to deal with the bureaucracy, as well as more in-depth guidance on the intricacies of the culture. If we choose to stay in this set, we will develop a fairly close-knit social circle, but it will have its limitations. Our conversations will often focus on the negative aspects of the host country, sometimes resulting in 'venting' sessions on how awful the locals are and what a drag it is to be living there or, to stay with a stereotype, how difficult it is to get decent household help. People complain that nothing is quite right and there is also plenty of criticism and bitching about other people in the set. This is because many of these social relationships are 'convenience' relationships – we are socializing with people we would not necessarily choose to be with at home.

Remaining exclusively in the expatriate environment can get you into a rut of circular arguments, without giving you the opportunity to learn something about the new culture or to adapt better by challenging your own attitudes and behavior. In this sense, you don't truly adapt because you don't develop an ability to function with confidence in more than one culture. Living in an expatriate bubble is similar to living on a small island, resulting in a preoccupation with minute issues and no consideration of the bigger picture. Managers who choose the expatriate set don't actively participate in whatever the country has to offer, they are not really part of anything – and they often suffer from stagnation and a feeling of waiting for something to happen.

The alternative to joining the cocktail set is to 'go native' and become involved in the local culture in an exclusive way. This happens with international managers who are extremely interested in the foreign culture and decide early on that they will focus their social and working life on host nationals. They despise the cocktail set and believe that interacting with compatriots will distract them from the 'real task' of doing a good job in the new place.

With this attitude, they may not even seek their compatriots' support at the beginning of the assignment. They will throw themselves into an intense phase of learning what the new place is about and what the characteristics and values of the different culture are. On the surface, this appears to be the right approach. However, it can result in an extreme attitude of idolization of everything about the new culture and devaluation of our own culture. In other words, the going native attitude implies that the host nationals have the right way of living, communicating and working, and that our own culture is inferior.

One manager in the oil industry reported the case of a colleague working in Jakarta who 'went native', did not perform very well and in the end was dismissed. He adapted too much to the slower pace in Indonesia and the lack of schedules and deadlines. Headquarters in Europe was not impressed!

It is easy to see how this attitude can have a negative effect: it can lead to an unbalanced view of the world but also, contrary to the manager's expectations, a lack of acceptance by the host nationals. A foreigner who tries to imitate the host nationals' behavior to an extreme degree will be treated with suspicion. Non-British people who become 'more British than the British' are not taken seriously and the same applies to any other exaggerated imitation.

Joining the cocktail set and going native are equally unhealthy in their extreme forms. The first is characterized by defensiveness against anything foreign, the second by defensiveness against our own culture. Both mindsets are one-sided and do not allow the development of true multiculturalism. This starts with understanding and accepting the values and perspectives of *both* cultures. It is a learning process that will ideally result in finding an effective compromise between our native way of doing things and a new, different way.

One manager reported the following experience:

"I thoroughly enjoyed Oman. Of course, there were invariably bad patches but it went well once we got a house and got settled. We tried to mix with the local Omanis and decided always to have very good holidays.

In Malaysia, it was much more difficult. My wife was at first not working and housing was a problem. I had a fantastic job and I couldn't come home in the evening and rave about my job when my wife was desperately looking for an occupation. Nevertheless, we had to move after two years in Malaysia and it was a disappointment for me to let go of my project and go to the new plant. The first year in Malaysia clearly was a problem but subsequently we adapted better. The way we adapted was to be active and have good holidays to make the most of it. We engaged in sports and sailing and were not too much concerned to save money but bought a four-wheel drive and a boat and so on to make it interesting. It is clear that it is very important to have good breaks and weekends to enjoy the experience. There are cases of people who just want to save money and then get overstressed and return before contract termination.

In contrast to that pattern, I enjoyed the fast social life, I had a large salary, a large social circle that was readily available and altogether a very exciting time. This was combined with a high degree of stimulation because of the diverse local culture."

This shows a manager in an expatriate circle but with a clear motivation to meet people from the host culture and a strong curiosity about the new place. This may be one way to achieve true multiculturalism: being relatively clear about our own cultural background but also sufficiently permeable in terms of learning different ways of thinking and behaving.

It is best to aim for a compromise – a combination of the cocktail set and going native approaches. In order to preserve our self-identity as part of our own national culture, we need to anchor ourselves in some way with people who come from the same cultural background. This gives us an emotional security zone, as well as practical advice. At the same time, this emotional security should be used to make steps forward into the new culture and to confront alternative ways of thinking and behaving.

Only a clear sense of identity can give us the confidence to question our own way of doing things and consider alternative approaches. Paradoxically, it is a strong sense of self and of personal values that allows us to expand and integrate new values. If we know who we are, we ultimately feel safe considering other ways of doing things and are not threatened by them. Managers with a weak sense of self feel threatened by the experience of 'otherness' – they put up defenses and withdraw into their national ways of doing things. A strong sense of self can also create openness: we are willing to learn new approaches that are more effective and integrate them into our previous ways of doing things. In this sense, international work can truly enrich our potential.

How to adapt

International managers find the following factors helpful when adapting to life abroad (Marx, 1996a). The suggestions are complemented by comments from individual managers who took part in the survey.

▲ Personality characteristics and attitudes such as patience, cooperative style, pragmatic orientation, flexibility, easy-going personality.

"I have been very flexible, getting used to things going wrong, but the most important thing is having an interest in people. Interpersonal skills are extremely important. The ability to adjust one's pace: for example, if one has to go through a lot of protocol, one has to have a lot of patience."

"I think I adapt well in different countries because I have a co-operative style. I get along with people and I do not believe in using my authority. I am not overly confrontational and am very pragmatic in my approach."

▲ Dealing with problems in a proactive way without being too self-aware or too self-analytical. This is an interesting point: at first sight it may contradict what we have said about being careful in cross-cultural situations, analyzing what is going on and being self-aware. What this advice points to is to the perfect balance between analysis, self-analysis and action. We have to be positive and have a 'can-do' attitude in order to overcome seemingly insurmountable problems. Some people can be put off their stroke by fairly minor hassles (the 'burnt toast' syndrome), whereas others only really get into gear when they are confronted by serious problems.

"I have seen several problem cases of people having difficulties in adaptation. The most drastic case was the wife of an international executive who committed suicide in Hong Kong because of the extreme social isolation."

"In my short-term international assignments, I adapted by biting my tongue, not patronizing and not using slang. I also tried to take nationality out of the business issues. On a personal level, it requires patience and understanding to adapt."

▲ Outside interests offer a comfort zone. It always helps to have a good range of interests outside work. This helps with general stress management, both at home and abroad. It provides somewhere to retreat to after difficult encounters during the working day. Some managers also mentioned the advantage of having strong religious beliefs.

▲ A real interest in the culture, the people and the customs. This goes beyond the superficial and means a clear affinity, curiosity and drive to understand more about the culture and its people. A real interest will result in a greater effort to come to a true understanding of the culture as well as achieving a balanced view of the positive and negative characteristics of the foreign country.

"I mainly socialized with my Asian colleagues in Hong Kong and so established very good friendships with people in the local community as opposed to having an expatriate life. I therefore never felt quite alienated but was relatively content right from the beginning. You do not feel alienation if you are in tune with the culture."

▲ Spending money and enjoying whatever activities the country has to offer. Some managers try to save too much money on international assignments, which can have negative effects on how they adapt: they are not willing to spend enough time and money to enjoy the opportunities of the host country.
▲ Enjoying a privileged lifestyle and a comfortable situation can also help to counteract potential stresses.

When asked about the most positive surprise, many managers in the survey answered "having a good lifestyle", such as:

▲ Comfortable and luxurious life
▲ Travel opportunities
▲ Enjoying the social life
▲ Developing a love for the culture and the place
▲ Opportunity to meet new people.

The importance of networking

Networking is an essential skill in business and it is even more important in an international context. A good networker will learn twice as fast about the local conditions and cross-cultural issues, while a bad networker will have a restricted view of what is going on around them and will obviously be less likely to establish relevant business contacts.

Networking is more important in countries that are more relationship oriented. In cultures that are more task than relationship oriented (northern Europe), networking may not be seen as important and therefore networking skills are not as essential. However, cultures that are relationship oriented (Asia, South America) are necessarily much more network oriented. In China, the need to work out the *guanxi* (business relationships) makes this more than evident.

International managers should therefore check whether their networking skills are good, sufficient or need improvement. An Austrian banker working for many years in Russia commented:

> *I am aware that as a consequence of this experience, I use networking much more effectively than before as I see the importance now much more clearly.*

Whereas in the past, comments like "so-and-so is such a networker" may have been derogatory, the positive effects of good networking skills are now indisputable. Networking not only improves the chances of finding a better job, it also makes it more likely that we will be effective at work. Chief executives with good networking skills are probably those who put the most interesting business deals together.

A good networker thinks in terms of systems – they assess the value of a contact in relation to their entire network. A bad networker assesses only the value to themselves. An attitude of "I can't see the point of spending time on lunches that have no immediate business objective" should be replaced with "I like to spread my net wide".

The fact that networking may be an area for all executives (national and international) to address is indicated by a research project on the development needs of top managers. I analyzed development needs on the basis of half-day psychological assessments of candidates for management positions. These positions were varied and included chief executive, project director, human resource director, investment strategist, IT services manager, sales director and finance director. The target group was 100 short-listed candidates, i.e. the best candidates for the positions advertised, but it was evident that there was a clear need to work on interpersonal skills. Among the top four development needs, three had an impact on the interpersonal area:

▲ *Interests/cognitive orientation*, such as lack of psychological understanding and lack of strategic orientation.
▲ *Interpersonal style*, such as interpersonal sensitivity and insufficient communication skills.
▲ *Emotional aspects*, such as anxiety and low social confidence or pessimism.

These results may be surprising, because few people would predict that senior managers could have weaknesses in these areas. However, the fact that more and more managers are using coaching consultants suggests that senior executives do have development needs and that this may be normal in the progression to a senior position.

Looking more closely at the top development needs, it is easy to imagine how they could affect the networking activities of an executive in the international arena: a lack of strategic orientation or psychological understanding, little interpersonal sensitivity and problems with social confidence will certainly not make it easy to be a good networker in a foreign environment.

We can differentiate between two essential components of networking: strategy and social skills.

The strategy of networking

Do you see your job responsibilities as very specific, focused and neatly defined, or do you take a much wider and flexible view? Does your task orientation result in fast and efficient completion, or do you look at the implications of your actions in more detail? Do you see task achievement as a straight line from A to B, or do you consider indirect but possibly more efficient routes?

Some managers take a holistic or systemic view, in that they see the interconnectedness of their actions. They know that they have a tough business issue to tackle, but they also look at the implications of getting there by various means. They look at the short- and long-term implications as well as those for people inside and outside the organization. While carrying out the task at hand, they never lose sight of the greater goals. Other managers, possibly those with a highly specialist or technical background, are trained to take a different and potentially narrower view. They concentrate on facts and figures and are not too concerned about the wider implications. Their view is not holistic or systemic and this will have a negative effect in an international setting.

Related to this is strategic planning. Many managers are extremely competent technically but find it difficult to make the jump from a technical role to a management position. One factor that is decisive for proceeding successfully to a higher management position is the ability to take a conceptual or strategic view: to be holistic, to look at long-term implications and to see the interconnectedness of events. This interconnectedness is partly factual in terms of hard business issues but, of course, it also has a 'softer' element, the people side. It is this combination of task and people orientation, together with a strategic view, that makes some managers more effective than others.

In terms of the people side, we may ask whether even highly successful executives take a sufficiently psychological view. Do they understand their impact on others as well as the way other people's behavior will affect them?

Certain incidents at senior management meetings create doubts about some executives' ability to take a psychological view. At one large company's senior international managers' conference, 90 executives were asked whether they believed that gender had an effect on the way products were perceived. As many as 40 percent did not believe that gender had an effect that should be considered in their marketing activities. Given the seniority of the group, this ignorance is a good example of a lack of psychological orientation. Similarly, a recent case showed that a European company found it easy to fire a senior executive in South America but much more difficult to understand the implications of this incident – the South American workforce perceived the decision makers in its European headquarters as callous, aggressive and not really interested in its employees, so the incident had a thoroughly demotivating effect.

Networking activities have to be strategically planned, particularly for executives who are not naturally inclined to use all contacts as potential business contacts. This is the case in more introvert (socially reserved) executives who would rather work on the factual task and take an analytical approach than be socially oriented and 'out and about'. These executives literally have to schedule networking activities into their weekly diaries.

Social skills

Socially skilled people perceive social situations accurately, are sensitive to how others respond to them and are flexible in their behavior, both verbally and non-verbally. Whether in China or the USA, it is important to gauge the appropriate space between two people in conversation, for example, or whether extended eye contact is seen as positive (instilling trust) or offensive (aggressive). There are commonly accepted ways of greeting or asking for favors and so on and a socially skilled person will be aware of these.

Executives who are ineffective in interactions can have problems at various levels: they may find it hard to understand what the other person wants, they may know what to do but feel too shy to do it, or their verbal and non-verbal behavior may be inconsistent and therefore may not have the desired impact.

As soon as a misunderstanding or an unfortunate social situation arises, it is important to assess exactly what went wrong. In a sense, you have to learn the new rules of the social game, what is appropriate and acceptable in the different culture.

A good example of rules or codes in social interaction is the use of humor in cross-cultural encounters. One can generally say that humor is always effective in interpersonal relations and can help to break down cross-cultural barriers. But what type of humor is acceptable in what kind of situation?

Examples abound of the use of humor backfiring in international business situations. It may not be acceptable or it may be misunderstood. For example, Germans find humor unacceptable in serious business situations. The French have a fairly sophisticated sense of humor and enjoy playing with language. British humor, on the other hand, is hard for outsiders to understand, because it tends to be self-deprecating and subtle. Americans are sometimes seen as lacking in humor, because they like to get on with things and do not always understand irony. Asian cultures, particularly the Chinese, appreciate humor in interactions, particularly if it is of the slapstick kind.

Humor requires careful observation and you have to learn the rules before you can join the game. Jean-Louis Barsoux, a specialist on humor in international business at INSEAD, advises people to wait until they have achieved a certain familiarity with their local counterparts before employing humor. If in doubt, don't joke!

Part Two

Conquering Culture Shock – Achieving Success

5

Understanding Business Cultures

Managers who are best able to conquer culture shock are often those who have a good understanding of different business cultures as well as cultural differences. This chapter provides a brief, pragmatic summary of some of the characteristics of the world's main business cultures, in areas such as workforce and society, business approach, organizational structure and a typical working day. These include Europe (Germany, France, the UK), the USA and China. They are inevitably shorthand and to some extent stereotypical, but they will offer valuable pointers to those who are working with people from these cultures, particularly in short-term situations such as some international teams.

Comprehensive overviews of these cultures and others can be found in Mole (1996), Hall and Hall (1990), Hampden-Turner and Trompenaars (1993) and Bond (1986).

Germany

I always find it interesting to look at airports, airport architecture, the way the services are handled and the general atmosphere to get a first impression of a country, its society and culture. Landing at Frankfurt airport, particularly the new Terminal 2, is impressive: it is glitzy and big, with glass walls, expensive materials, generous planning and a logical layout – everything you would expect in Germany. However, it takes ages to get through passport control: every single passport is scrutinized and put through an electronic detection system, resulting in large queues of people waiting to get to the luggage area and out of the airport. Is this a colossal system that does not seem to be terribly efficient at times, or is efficiency simply defined in a different way? Bearing all this in mind, how can we succinctly categorize the German business culture?

Workforce/society

▲ There is a solid education system (mainly state education).
▲ The workforce is well educated (many people up to university level).
▲ Currently, there is high unemployment, particularly among well-educated people.
▲ There is a focus on learning foreign languages – German employees are expected to be fluent in at least one foreign language.
▲ Some managers have international experience, but there is still quite a national outlook within German business.
▲ Germany has a broad middle class with a good standard of living and a high quality of life is seen as extremely important (see working times).
▲ Moving employees to other locations is difficult, at national level as well as internationally. Because of the *Länder* system and a North/South divide, employees do not move easily. This can make it difficult to expand a German company internationally.

Business atmosphere and approach

▲ Employees like to have clear job descriptions but thereafter prefer little interference in their work.

▲ German companies are quite hierarchical. Their task approach is relatively structured, with the advantage of predictability and the disadvantage of rigidity. There is a strong focus on technical quality and professional excellence.

▲ Speed is not as important as taking a thorough approach. German companies are known for taking a long-term view: they may have a longer planning phase, but implement quickly, with possibly fewer problems than business cultures with a short-term orientation.

▲ Germans are sequential time planners; they dislike interruptions or changes of schedule.

▲ Long working hours are not necessarily interpreted as high job commitment, but rather as not being clever enough to finish your work within normal hours.

▲ Punctuality is highly valued and is seen as a sign of respect.

▲ Germans separate private and business life; they have long holidays and it is not the norm to take business phone calls on holiday.

▲ There is still a relatively long-term view of employment, suggesting that employees do not like to jump from job to job.

▲ Work is considered to be important in the German culture and there is a strong personal identification with the job.

▲ As a consequence of their long-term view, Germans often do not like change and show a low tolerance of ambiguity. This can make dealing with them difficult in an international context.

Business communication

▲ German business culture is relatively formal. First names are not used and the traditionally polite form *Sie* is used instead of the more informal *Du*.

▲ The business tone is serious and can be fairly direct, up to the point of being very assertive. Do not make the mistake of using jokes, as humor is not welcome in a business setting.

▲ Germans have a direct and task-oriented approach.

▲ Meetings follow a clear agenda and are dealt with in a decisive and formal way.

▲ There is a natural respect for authority and compliance; eccentricity is not tolerated.

▲ Politeness and good manners are always expected.

▲ German business culture is a little staid, particularly at senior level.

▲ Advertising works by giving a wealth of information and statistics about a product as opposed to projecting an image (in both creativity and design).

Organizational structure and leadership

▲ Public corporations and large limited companies have a supervisory board that appoints the management board (*Vorstand*) and makes the important decisions.

▲ Germans like decisive leadership. Leaders are respected because of their technical/professional expertise.

▲ There is no dominant elite in Germany as the education system is fairly meritocratic.

▲ There is a strong identification with the firm and the profession.

▲ It is important to be well educated and to use academic titles in business.

▲ Germans recognize that they have to develop a stronger service culture. In this respect, US companies often have a clear advantage.

Business wear

▲ Business attire is relatively formal: men always wear a jacket but not always a full suit.

Working day

▲ Start early, work intensively and go home early summarizes the German approach.
▲ Germans like to eat lunch as their main meal.
▲ In the evenings, employees prefer to go straight home and don't mix business with pleasure. This approach makes business entertaining difficult.

Weaknesses in German business

▲ The skills of networking and its importance are not sufficiently focused on, compared to other countries.

France

Landing at Charles de Gaulle Airport is like being in a 1960s science fiction movie. Its interesting, space-age design illustrates France's affinity for technical advances and modernist architecture and the importance of engineering within its culture. But is design more important than efficiency? To the newcomer, the airport is slightly confusing as you have the impression of running round in circles. However, there is no doubt that there is always an interesting and surprising angle to consider.

Workforce/society

▲ There is a strong education system, with a particular emphasis on mathematics and engineering and with elite schools and universities (*Grandes Ecoles, Polytechniques*).
▲ The workforce is well educated.
▲ Unemployment is high but the situation is set to improve.
▲ Learning foreign languages is reasonably important. There is still quite a national outlook.
▲ There is a moderate amount of international mobility.

Business atmosphere and approach

▲ The system is very hierarchical.
▲ The French have a flexible task approach.
▲ The approach is dynamic and innovative.
▲ Accountants are not as highly valued as in, for example, the UK.
▲ Business takes a long-term view.
▲ Time planning is more synchronic, with many interruptions and easy changes from one task to the next.
▲ Working hours are relatively long (because of lunch).
▲ Punctuality is valued, but people are always expected to be 10 to 15 minutes late for a social occasion.
▲ Business lunches of two to three hours are the norm and discussion of business issues is only allowed over dessert.
▲ Hard work and professionalism are seen as important but workaholism as negative.
▲ There is a moderate orientation towards change and a particular affinity for technological advances.

Business communication

▲ Communication is relatively formal (no first names, particularly not to the boss).
▲ The approach is intellectual, indirect, sophisticated: verbal fluency reflects your level of education and it is important to demonstrate this in a business conversation.
▲ The priority is to establish relationships first, then get on with the tasks.
▲ Meetings consist of ongoing discussions that do not necessarily reach a conclusion.
▲ There is a high respect for authority, based on competence.
▲ There is a strong elite network: many of the senior directors come from the elite universities (*Grandes Ecoles*), constituting a close-knit business network.

Organizational structure and leadership

▲ Some companies have a two-tier system. The concept of the
   patron is most important – senior executives are given a great deal
   of respect.
▲ Authoritative leadership is tolerated and employees are supposed
   to follow.
▲ There is an intellectual approach to business with a great deal of
   brainstorming and discussions.
▲ Employees are expected to stay longer with the company,
   compared to the USA or the UK.

Business wear

▲ The approach is formal, elegant and relatively fashionable.

Working day

▲ The day is very long (with late working hours) because of the
   extended lunch break.

Weaknesses in French business

▲ There is possibly a lack of diversity, produced by the elite system.
▲ There is a need to become more international.

UK

'Arriving at Heathrow is like arriving in a third world country,' commented a self-critical British friend. The main Heathrow building
with its three terminals always seems to be in a state of chaos with
permanent attempts at improvement, leaving the traveler in a similar
state of confusion. Although Heathrow has improved dramatically
over the years and has extensive shopping facilities, its rather slapdash

approach towards airport architecture may reflect the UK's 'layperson' approach. The British are pragmatic and have a low-key attitude to adversity: they don't get too upset and may not seek perfectionism at all costs; they are also prepared to change and to be flexible. This may be one of their strong points when it comes to business.

Workforce/society

▲ The education system could be considered shaky by continental standards, with a highly criticized and inefficient state school system and private schools that educate a small percentage of children, mainly from affluent families.

▲ University education is not considered as important as in most European countries. There is now a shift towards greater appreciation of academic degrees and a larger university intake.

▲ Oxford and Cambridge degrees are still quite important in career terms, similar to having been to an elite private school. The traditional 'old boy' network (starting at prep school, continuing through secondary school and university) still operates, although there is probably more diversity now than some decades ago.

▲ The advantage of the system in terms of career planning and development is its flexibility.

▲ The UK currently has a strong employment market.

▲ British business is characterized by its international outlook, with quite a number of managers having good international experience (though probably still as a consequence of colonial times).

▲ The traditional class system with distinct upper and working classes is still noticeable and there remains a focus on speaking with the 'right' accent, although regional accents are better accepted than they used to be.

▲ The British workforce is characterized by high mobility, both nationally and internationally.

Business atmosphere and approach

▲ Similar to the USA, a pragmatic and flexible attitude prevails.
▲ Strict job descriptions are not always necessary.
▲ The flexibility of approach may result in a lack of perfectionism.
▲ The main focus is on getting things done; while speed is important, it is probably not as important as in the USA.
▲ A short-term view: the focus is on shareholder value, and the lack of longer-term planning means that the business approach is often reactive and there can be frequent changes of strategy.
▲ Time planning is flexible (something between sequential and synchronic).
▲ British managers have the longest working hours in Europe. There is a macho attitude, suggesting that it is positive to stay as long as possible at your desk. British managers have short holidays compared to other Europeans.
▲ There is a significant overlap between private and business life. Business breakfasts, lunches and dinners are common. Business entertaining can take place on the golf course, at tennis, cricket and rugby matches or at the opera.
▲ Employees take a relatively short-term view of employment, probably an effect of the bad recession in the late 1980s.
▲ The British are fairly change oriented and have the advantage of tolerating ambiguity.

Business communication

▲ Communication is relatively informal (first names are usually used, except for very senior executives in some organizations).
▲ The culture is definitely humor oriented. Small talk and good social skills are highly valued.
▲ Communication is not direct.
▲ It is important not to 'rock the boat' and to be team oriented.
▲ There is no automatic respect for authority and a certain irreverence is notable in many organizations.
▲ The system is relatively democratic, with flat hierarchies.
▲ Eccentricity is valued to a degree.

▲ Politeness is important.

▲ Time is spent on small talk before approaching business issues.

▲ The UK is particularly good at advertising, with funky artwork and witty dialogue. In this area, it is much more creative than many other countries.

Organizational structure and leadership

▲ There is a one-tier system: the board of directors makes the decisions and is headed by a chairman and chief executive. Large companies have non-executive directors.

▲ Accountants are very important in British business (many chief executives have an accountancy background).

▲ Leadership is team oriented and not authoritarian, both in developing teams and in coaching managers. The need for 'soft' skills and team leadership is always emphasized.

▲ Meetings are often informal but reasonably structured; consensus is important.

▲ The British emphasis on understatement and reserve is evident in business meetings. This reserve is sometimes interpreted as a lack of interest or standoffishness by foreigners.

▲ There is a dislike of intellectual issues in business.

Business wear

▲ Full suits are always worn (tailoring is important), except in some creative and IT companies, where casual designer wear is more appropriate.

▲ Foreigners often stumble over the expression 'black tie dinner' and turn up wearing a black tie – in fact, it signifies formal evening wear.

Working day

▲ Working hours are long.
▲ Long lunches are becoming popular again with the renewed affluence in business.
▲ Employees often go for drinks after work, showing their ease at mixing business with pleasure.

USA

Landing at San Francisco airport is at first a pleasant experience – a great location for an airport and a smooth transition through immigration; there are efforts to show off the Californian flora and a distinctly personal touch in a greeting from the city's mayor. However, this personal greeting is a continuous tape and when you have to hear it for the third time in three minutes, you are getting slightly tired of this noise pollution – is this a symptom of the automatized, 'have a nice day' service orientation in the USA?

Workforce/society

▲ There is a moderately good education system, although many state schools and universities do not achieve sufficiently high quality.
▲ Many managers have a university education, but the particular university is important. There are only a few elite universities.
▲ There is no strong focus on learning a foreign language.
▲ Despite the international expansion of many US businesses, organizations are plagued by a high failure rate in their international managers. This may be due to insufficient preparation or the general lack of an international outlook.
▲ The standard of living is very high and managers expect the same standards when moving abroad (US expatriates are notoriously demanding in terms of the standard of their accommodation and the need for power showers, etc.).
▲ There is a great deal of mobility nationally – Americans seem to move around much more than Europeans.

▲ There is high staff turnover, as employees seem to change jobs on a more regular basis compared to Europe.

Business atmosphere and approach

▲ The culture is highly individualist, which may make real teamwork difficult.
▲ The society is meritocratic and achievement oriented.
▲ There is a preference for flat hierarchies, although there is no real questioning of the superior. Irreverent behavior towards superiors is not encouraged!
▲ Americans are tough time planners: they created the time-is-money attitude and they can be seen as pushy and aggressive.
▲ Excessive working hours are encouraged, although their effectiveness cannot always be established.
▲ Americans created the idea of business breakfasts and business lunches; it seems that every minute is used for deal making.
▲ American executives are often accused of short-termism and a lack of a longer-term perspective.
▲ There is a high service orientation: most European countries try to imitate the service approach of US companies.

Business communication

▲ Superficially, business communication is relatively informal. First names are used and casual dress is encouraged if no formal business meetings are being attended (the Americans were responsible for the introduction of 'dress down Fridays').
▲ The business tone is factual and direct and Americans are frequently admired for their excellent presentation skills. At international conferences, they are usually the slickest presenters. They are trained early on to be articulate and to present their own and their business's achievements.
▲ Americans take a task-oriented and extremely positive approach.
▲ Meetings have a clear agenda and organizations typically communicate extensively with their employees in writing.

▲ Despite the flat hierarchies, Americans are relatively compliant to those in authority. As with Germany, eccentricity is not particularly tolerated.

▲ New ideas are always welcomed and fresh approaches encouraged. After all, the USA is a country of pioneers.

Organizational structure and leadership

▲ Americans like decisive leadership.

▲ There is a small business elite, coming from the best universities and business schools. The alumni system in universities is well established and networking is highly encouraged. On the other hand, the USA is the classic country of the self-made.

▲ High salaries are extremely important in defining social status. Salaries ('How much do you make?') are not seen as a taboo subject for discussion, unlike in Europe.

Business wear

▲ Business wear is relatively formal for business meetings, more casual otherwise and on 'dress down' days.

Working day

▲ Start early and go home late summarizes the American approach: long working hours are encouraged.

▲ Lunches may be sandwiches or working occasions.

▲ Business and pleasure are mixed, but possibly in a more structured way, for example only at certain times, compared to cultures that are more strongly relationship oriented.

Weaknesses in US business

▲ The orientation is short term.
▲ It is questionable whether real teamwork is possible in this highly individualistic culture.
▲ The relatively high failure rate in international managers may change with a stronger international orientation and better preparation of more managers.

China

Beijing Airport, 1992, on holiday – landing in a daze after a harrowing flight. Glad to be alive and being processed through the airport – there is a clear separation in the treatment of foreigners and PRC Chinese. Fortunately, I am met by an American friend who is a fluent Chinese speaker and has lived in China for years – an example of a translator with the right links whom every western businessperson needs in China.

Workforce/society

▲ There are few well-educated managers or general employees.
▲ There is a high demand for managers who are university educated, particularly those with degrees from international universities or those who have worked with international companies.
▲ The recently strong economy is slowing down and there is high unemployment among the uneducated workforce.
▲ There is a focus on developing a strong achievement motivation.
▲ Confucian values have a strong influence: loyalty to family and group, focus on education and acquisition of skills, etc. Hierarchy is seen to be natural and there is a sense of the complementarity of relationships (Bond, 1986).
▲ Developing the right connections (*guanxi*) is important.
▲ With the improved economic situation, there is extensive movement of the population into industrialized cities.
▲ Highly educated Chinese managers can ask for premium salaries.

Business atmosphere and approach

▲ There is a clear entrepreneurial attitude in the Chinese culture. It is generally seen as more positive to run your own business than to be employed by a large multinational. This means that multinationals have to consider carefully how to attract and keep the best managers.

▲ Traditionally, the system is very hierarchical and structured but is also family oriented. Chinese business cultures can have a paternalist feel.

▲ Speed is important and adapting to western styles of production is seen as essential.

▲ Chinese are synchronic time planners; they can juggle demands and are extremely flexible.

▲ They are highly committed and work long hours, particularly when building up their own businesses.

▲ For both historical and economic reasons, leisure is not as important as in western cultures.

▲ There is a strong overlap between private life and business life: the focus is on relationship building and the development of trust.

▲ There is a relatively long-term view in business, but not necessarily in employment.

Business communication

▲ The leadership style is direct and authoritarian. Orders are given and complied with. The top-down tradition makes it difficult for subordinates to be proactive, but the culture may be changing in organizations that are operating internationally.

▲ The Chinese have a fast and task-oriented approach, despite their need to establish relationships with business partners.

▲ Meetings do have an agenda, although business communication is much more indirect compared to western approaches.

▲ There is a natural respect for authority and the focus is on harmony as opposed to disagreement and open argument in groups.

▲ Politeness and good manners are highly valued.
▲ A sense of humor is welcomed.
▲ An appreciation of food is important.

Organizational structure and leadership

▲ The business structure is hierarchical, with the leader having natural authority.
▲ Because of the speed of economic development, there is not necessarily a strong identification with the firm and good managers may easily be poached by other companies.
▲ Education is seen as highly important in Chinese culture and academic titles are often used.

Business wear

▲ The style is relatively formal and becoming more westernized.

Working day

▲ Working hours are long because of the overlap of business and social relationships.

Weaknesses in Chinese business

▲ There is a lack of an international approach and knowledge of western business methods.
▲ There is a shortage of highly educated managers, particularly those with international experience.

Another look at cultural differences

Business cultures have a particularly strong influence on international mergers and international teams. Before we look at this in more detail, it may be useful to think about some other factors that have an impact on cultural differences.

Thinking style and language

Different cultures have different styles of thinking that affect the way they see business. For example, Dr Chua Fook Kee of the National University of Singapore pointed out to me that the Chinese language lacks the grammar to signal the subjunctive mood and this may affect the way in which Chinese deal with hypothetical situations and discussions. For example, while they may be willing to contemplate plausible conditions (such as 'if I were as rich as Bill Gates'), they may not be prepared to think of implausible conditions (such as 'if I were Bill Gates'). This may contribute to the great pragmatism of Chinese businesspeople.

Another example is the French language and its preference for *bon mots*, alliteration and allusion. This has a great influence in business. In discussion, it is important to converse with style. Rather than merely stating facts, the elegance of language demonstrates the manager's education and cultural background, factors valued in French society. A business negotiation is therefore not a mere discussion but a discourse (*discours*).

The German language is literal and precise. Germans like to put issues into their 'proper' context, to give all the facts and figures and to construct a logical argument, supported by examples. To some cultures this seems a rather long-winded approach and one that is particularly evident in the German style of report writing. Following German standards, an author's intelligence is reflected in the complexity of sentence construction. This is in contrast to the British tradition, where intelligent writing is reflected in making it simple and accessible.

In order to understand other cultures, therefore, it is not sufficient to be able to translate – you have to comprehend the subtleties and connotations of the language. Walter Hasselkus, the German chief executive of Rover, gave a good example of this when he remarked: "When the British say that they have a 'slight' problem, I know that it has to be taken seriously." There are numerous examples of misunderstandings between American English and British English, even though they are, at root, the same language.

Philosophy

Our native country's philosophical tradition has a strong impact on the way we think and operate, although we may not be able to quote the exact theorems behind it. The most obvious difference is between the Anglo-Saxon philosophy and the continental idealist tradition and the impact of both on our thinking.

Anglo-Saxon philosophy is influenced by the empiricist tradition and its main representatives, John Locke and David Hume. This tradition, with its focus on data and factual verification, has resulted in a number-oriented, highly pragmatic approach to doing business (compare the number of accountants in the UK to those in Germany); consequently the theoretical background of management decisions is not as important as the statistical findings supporting them.

In contrast, the philosophy in both France and Germany (e.g. Hegel, Kant, Descartes) is characterized by idealist theories. These do not focus on empirical data but on the philosophy of ideas. As a consequence, models, theories of management and intellectual debates about hypothetical questions are seen to be as important as a focus on factual data. This can result in frustrating management situations. For example, British or American managers trying to get the task done on the basis of convincing statistics are irritated when French managers start debating the models behind the decision and the theoretical issues.

Confucianism has had an impact in China for about 2000 years, particularly in relation to the most important social relationships – the five cardinal relations of sovereign and subject, father and son, elder brother and younger brother, husband and wife, friend and friend. Its influence on the cultural dimension of collectivism seems evident. But how strong is the Confucian tradition in today's China or for Hong Kong or Singaporean Chinese? These societies are changing at a tremendous pace and the outcome of the fusion of eastern and western values is difficult to predict.

Which international business partners work best together?

Some years ago, the Harris Research Institute in London asked 1500 top managers from Belgium, Germany, Spain, France, Italy, the Netherlands and the UK the question: 'What do you think of your foreign colleagues?' The results were surprising, particularly with regard to the Germans: 25 percent of senior managers in Europe believe that it is easiest to work with Germans. Next in the list were the French (favored by 17 percent) and the British (10 percent).

This result is surprising in view of the fact that Germans are not necessarily regarded as the most 'likable' nation. However, one German manager believes that it is explained by the fact that in the complexity of international business, their systematic task approach is often very helpful. This suggests that the Germans – with their structured approach, direct interaction style and tendency to look at problems – are easier to deal with in an international context, because the way they work may be more transparent than that of the other Europeans this survey addressed.

International mergers

Many companies at an international level are the result of mega-mergers between already large organizations, and this trend is set to continue.

The human side of mergers has to be resolved early on if the new organization wants to achieve maximum performance and market competitiveness. Whether the merger is a friendly combination of companies or a hostile takeover, a number of problems seem to be inherent in both scenarios. What happens in mergers can be illustrated in various ways:

▲ Group dynamics
▲ Compatability of corporate and national cultures
▲ Culture shock or the shock of change.

Consideration of each of these areas exposes certain typical stages in a merger.

Group dynamics

We experience the effect of group dynamics every day. We all belong to various social, political or organizational groups and these form part of our identity. Who we are is to a large extent defined by where we are or the group to which we belong. These groups are not arbitrary but chosen, because we like to belong to the best or superior group. Consequently, we discriminate between different groups according to their value and status and normally see our group as better than others. As a consequence, we differentiate between the 'in group' (our group) and the 'out group' (the others) – we develop an 'us and them' attitude.

This results in the 'out group' being stereotyped, particularly in hostile takeovers when there is a realistic fear of being swamped and marginalized by the dominant organization. But even in less aggressive circumstances, we have normal concerns, such as:

▲ Is Organization X going to win, that is, determine our new culture and corporate strategy?
▲ Is my job safe or will I be replaced by someone from the other company?
▲ Will I have to change my working style dramatically in order to survive?
▲ Should I simply put my head down and try to 'swim with the tide' or can I play an active part in shaping the new organization?
▲ Can I actually work closely with the people from Organization X?

Compatibility of corporate and national cultures

There are numerous definitions of corporate culture, perhaps the most appropriate being 'the way we do things around here' (Deal and Kennedy, 1982). Culture is an organization's social 'glue' and generates a feeling of 'us'. It is a shared system of meanings and represents the basis for communication and mutual understanding. The main functions of corporate culture are internal integration and coordination. If these two functions are not fulfilled, the efficiency of an organization will be significantly reduced.

Differences in organizational culture are also reflected in variations in management style. Schoenberg (1997) found that differences in management style had a negative impact on performance in cross-border acquisitions. He studied 129 cross-border acquisitions originating in the UK and analyzed the performance of these companies five years after the acquisition. Attitude towards risks was seen as the critical component in management style influencing subsequent company performance. Schoenberg strongly recommended that organizations carry out a due diligence study of management culture in addition to the traditional financial and commercial due diligence. This should particularly focus on the risk orientation of the two merging companies: do they share a similar focus on research and development? What are their investment profiles in terms of risk? Do they have a similar timeframe for decision making?

Even in the best of organizations, senior managers do not always behave in a rational manner and they tend to take a variety of attitudes to cultural differences. These can range from 'our way is the best and others just have to follow' through 'cultural differences are a myth' to 'every culture does things differently and we should try to create a new, hybrid culture'.

Comparing organizational cultures when contemplating an acquisition will allow you to determine how great the overlap is, how easy it will be to merge them and how long this is likely to take.

Culture shock or shock of change?

International mergers can produce a similar process of culture shock to that of individual managers facing new cultures. Employees of the organizations being merged may initially take a positive view if they believe the often encouraging press coverage. However, they quickly plunge into a period of culture shock, characterized by difficulty in dealing with the uncertainty and general disorientation as well as a fear of loss or actual deprivation in professional terms. There is a certain inertia when organizations are undergoing a merger – a great deal of time is spent on organizational politics and this results in performance problems and a lack of focus on the external environment and competitors.

Eventually – depending on how successful senior managers are in dealing with psychological issues – employees may develop a more realistic outlook in the recovering phase and start integrating the 'foreign' values into their own value system. The search for compromise between values, behavior and attitudes has started and will possibly be completed in the adaptation phase, characterized by a consolidation of the new culture. Given the fact that business itself is becoming more global, international mergers can often produce a much more creative culture, with an increased ability to perform in a complex marketplace. The ultimate task of senior management is to turn the diversity of the merged organizations and the related culture shock into a competitive advantage. Sadly, very few business leaders seem to be able to achieve this, as the high failure rate in cross-cultural mergers suggests.

How do organizations reach this final adaptation stage and break through the culture shock? Whatever the differences between the companies may be, awareness and acknowledgment of the potential problems is the first step towards adaptation, as can be seen in the adaptation of individuals. In terms of combining different cultures, we have to recognize the different cultural dimensions (as outlined in Chapter 3) as well as the different corporate cultures.

The 1998 Daimler Benz/Chrysler merger is going to be an interesting example to observe. One of the differences in these two organizational and national cultures concerns their attitudes towards pay and benefits for their chief executives. As the *Wall Street Journal* (26 May 1998) observed, there are huge differences in executive packages between the German and American CEOs. As the article explained, Germans are more concerned with equality in pay and focus on salary differentials, whereas US companies are not really concerned with this issue, being much more individualist in focus. In terms of cultural dimensions, this may reflect the higher individualism of the USA versus the more collectivist approach in Germany.

Originally hailed as a 'merger of equals', the series of events that have followed since 1998 points in a different direction. One of the essential questions, as with any merger, was not where production would take place but who would have the top executive positions in the newly formed organization. In November 1998, DaimlerChrysler announced the names of the top 250 senior executives immediately below the board. It stressed that these people were drawn fairly evenly from both sides. However, half a year later, the difficulty of integrating business cultures and people became more and more obvious when many key senior Chrysler executives departed. While Juergen Schrempp (of Daimler-Benz) and Bob Eaton (of Chrysler) are still co-chairmen, Bob Eaton's retirement in 2001 confirms the teutonic dominance of the merger.

At the same time, the current media coverage shows that US investors are becoming more concerned about the different corporate cultures, despite the merged company's initial good results. In addition, in October 2000 DaimlerChrysler reported a significant fall in profits because of the losses made in the US Chrysler Group. A clash of business cultures was to be expected, however, as we have seen in this chapter. Ideally, integration needs to be planned carefully on the basis of prior organizational/cultural audits.

Examples of integration on the basis of international teams are given below and in Chapter 9.

The issue of corporate and national cultures is often addressed in team workshops. Understanding each other's backgrounds (whether corporate or cultural) and agreeing on 'ways we will be doing things around here' can be the basis for a new, much more effective organization.

The challenge of international teams

Culturally diverse teams can be very effective in international business. However, in order to make this happen, some groundwork has to be done. The most important rule is to spend some time on team processes, especially in the initial stages of the team's formation.

I recently prepared a team workshop aimed at helping a British/American team work more effectively together. This team needed to improve its transatlantic communication. A preliminary assessment of its difficulties showed the following:

▲ Excessive stereotyping
▲ A need to understand each other's cultures better
▲ A lack of openness and communication
▲ The 'culture factor' was seen as an overused excuse for not being able to get the job done.

The subsequent team workshop specified the differences in working styles shown in Table 10.

Table 10 Perceived differences of US and British team members

British view of Americans	American view of British
Too directive	Too consensus driven
Too aggressive	Too defensive
Too fast	Quality rather than quantity oriented
Focusing on the possible but not thinking about obstacles	Very bureaucratic
'Cowboys shooting from the hip'	Focusing on negatives
	Their long-term planning required longer implementation and they were risk averse
	Taking too many holidays
	Having shorter working days
	Inflexible
	Sluggish

On the basis of these perceived differences, we challenged organizational and cultural perceptions, undertook various team exercises, analyzed differences in cross-cultural dimensions and checked whether the two teams really spoke the same language.

Recommended steps for creating an effective international team are as follows:

▲ Decide on a common working language and develop agreed goals.
▲ Develop the right balance between joint team meetings and the work and communication in between (if team members are in different locations, decide on the mode of communication, such as fax and e-mail, and appropriate times).
▲ Spend sufficient time sharing the rationale and objectives with the team.
▲ Choose the right leader – in a technical, interpersonal and intercultural sense. For example, in Germany the team leader is usually the person with the best technical knowledge; in Italy the team leader is often the person with the highest status in the organization or the department.
ზ ▲ Respect and acknowledge the influence of culture and offer support and training in cross-cultural differences.
▲ Ensure balanced participation. In some cultures interruptions are the norm, whereas in others they are unacceptable. For example, with Chinese or Japanese team members, the team leader often has to ask explicitly for their opinion because free-floating discussions and contributions are not encouraged. Choose a team leader with the necessary intercultural skills who will ensure participation from all members, both in discussion and decision making.
ɤ ▲ Work through conflicts rather than avoiding them. Conflicts are part of team development and should be considered as steps on the path to better performance.
ɤ ▲ Use facilitators if necessary to establish group and intercultural skills at the beginning.
ɤ ▲ Allow time for discussing and reviewing group processes. Increased awareness, interpersonal understanding and sensitivity are essential ingredients of high performance.

Evaluating team members' cultural effectiveness

Most managers find it quite difficult to gauge the international effectiveness of team members on the basis of their usual behavior in meetings. It is therefore useful to look at behavior in terms of positive and negative indicators of cross-cultural sensitivity, adaptability to new situations and communication skills. These are listed in the checklist below.

Checklist of behavioral indicators

Cross-cultural sensitivity

Positive indicators
▲ Shows different cultural perspectives (e.g. they may think…, it may be that…).
▲ Takes an abstract/attributional approach (asks about cause, motivation, possible reasons for behavior).
▲ Presents many alternative strategies (note whether with or without 'cultural slant').
▲ Relates to own experience with the same or other culture.
▲ Shows concrete, factual knowledge of different lifestyles, thinking styles, cultures.

Negative indicators
▲ Gives simplified solutions without perspective taking.
▲ Stereotypic/ethnocentric stance (racist comments, own national solutions presented as the right ones).
▲ Defeatist approach (if this doesn't work, there's nothing we can do).

Adaptability to new situations

Positive indicators
▲ Can think on their feet in unfamiliar situations.
▲ Reacts fast to different perspectives, is flexible and open, i.e. can change way of thinking (accepting others' arguments, following up other ideas even if these are contradictory to their own).
▲ Asks questions about other culture, trying to get more information.
▲ Attempts to resolve the issue.

Negative indicators
▲ Appears insecure or even irritated when dealing with vague or 'softer'/psychological management issues.

Communication/relationships skills/people orientation

Positive indicators
▲ Reacts fast to others' comments (does not ignore any participants, acknowledges the value of everyone's contribution).
▲ Shows understanding of others' position.
▲ Does not interrupt others or talk too much.
▲ Good non-verbal communication (eye contact, body posture).
▲ Does not show any irritation despite time pressure.

Negative indicators
▲ Interrupts others or talks too much.

6

Frequent Flyers to Dual Careers

In the 1980s, executives may have thrived on a macho attitude and a separation of work and personal life, but in the 1990s, most take a more realistic view and have a more balanced orientation. There is no doubt that work performance can improve with happiness in your personal life and, inversely, can dramatically decline as a result of personal problems. It is therefore important to review the various scenarios that international managers may experience in relation to their social and personal lives and consider how to deal with them effectively. These relate to relationships and the experiences of partners and children, as well as the problems inherent in short-term international work and what to consider when coming home.

Swinging singles

Jonathan was a highly educated British manager who had been transferred to the company's Singaporean subsidiary on an expatriate package, luxury accommodation and club membership. As regional director, his job involved frequent traveling outside Singapore. I knew him from the UK and I bumped into him in a supermarket in Singapore after not having seen him for several years.

It was clear that he enjoyed every moment of his international life. He was hard working and on a high note in his career: he had just reached director level with greater responsibility and his new job was interesting and varied. He was enjoying the materialistic rewards of his job and his expatriate status in an Asian country. A strong extravert, he had joined several sports and social clubs and he also had a string of Singaporean girlfriends.

The lifestyle of many single executives in international assignments, particularly in so-called expatriate paradises, is often similar to the above description. There is a high pitch about these lifestyles: they are adrenalin-driven in terms of job responsibilities and in terms of social life. These types of managers are rarely ever on their own following some solitary pursuits, they are always 'out there', clubbing, meeting more people and simply having fun. It is a wonderful lifestyle for a limited time, but there is also something very artificial about it. As with the cocktail set described in Chapter 4, this lifestyle is highly transitory. People you socialize with come and go all the time and your social life is mainly focused on parties and meeting lots of different people. As quantity has priority over quality, these friendships are often superficial and non-committal.

The absence of the normal social control is liberating but can also result in excesses of various kinds. Anybody who has worked internationally can easily think of incidents that support this. And many host nationals can report excessive behavior by expatriates. In the case of Nick Leeson, the man who brought down Barings Bank, one such excess was allegedly taking down his trousers in a nightclub in Singapore.

Sometimes the lack of social control and norms will make it difficult for managers to decide what is acceptable and unacceptable. Alternatively, they may develop exaggerated self-confidence and become brash, believing that they can do anything they like.

The flipside is the isolation and loneliness that many single international managers experience. They feel alienated and, because they don't have the advantage of being able to discuss deeper personal feelings with a partner, it may take them longer to accept the changes and demands of a long-term assignment.

One manager I talked to reported this explicitly. He had worked for several years in the Middle East and found himself in the rather unusual situation of being the only single manager in an expatriate circle. Although most families seemed very welcoming, he was something of a 'mascot': someone to invite for dinner or Sunday lunch or to organize sports activities. However, he was isolated because he had a different personal life from everyone else.

This can be compared with the experience of an aid worker who recently returned after several years working in Sudan:

> *"It is good to be back in terms of being anonymous in a large city. In Sudan, I was the only white person around and therefore I was always seen and treated as someone unique and peculiar. It is wonderful not to have that 'standing out' experience and to dive into the anonymity of a large city. "*

Single expatriates have the advantage of having more time to enjoy the many social activities that are offered. However, being a swinging single is also hard work if you want to establish and maintain a close network of real friends, not just people to have a party with.

Honeymoons and nightmares in relationships

International work can make or break relationships. The thrill of the new environment and the opportunity to see each other in a different context can bring couples much closer together. In addition, overcoming the challenges that a change brings, whether on a long-term foreign assignment or a short-term stint abroad, can deepen relationships. It is also an opportunity to break the well-established routines that couples get into. In the same way that international experience can broaden individuals' interests and give them a new 'lease of life', it can give couples an entire new way of living together.

I found several examples of managers who went abroad with their partners and decided to get married. As one executive commented:

> *"We became closer and, as a consequence, decided to get married while working in Spain. "*

Accompanying partners often develop new interests abroad, particularly if they have more time or are not working and enjoy what the new country can offer. A British manager working in France reported:

"My wife absolutely loved the experience in Paris. She was able to socialize in a much more international circle and she also developed a new interest in the history of art and pursued it to quite an intense degree. "

The spouse and the family are becoming more prominent in international work. Organizations have realized that they have to take a much more holistic view of international managers – they have to consider personal issues if they want their international managers to succeed. Ways in which the most progressive companies help their managers will be discussed in Chapter 8.

Organizations may at last have realized that the happiness of the spouse contributes to the success of an international assignment. Research has shown that how the spouse adapts is a powerful predictor of a successful assignment abroad. As early as 1972, Stoner, Aram and Rubin showed that support from a spouse was an essential factor in the performance of international managers. Spouses who were positive about international assignments from the very beginning seemed to have a beneficial effect on performance. In contrast, managers whose spouses were negative about moving overseas received the worst performance appraisals. It seems that the spouse's support acts as a strong buffer against the stress of international transition.

Unfortunately, not every married manager has the benefit of such support. Some researchers have concluded that marriage is a liability to those working overseas. There are many cases where relationships drift apart. This is especially true when a relationship is already 'on the rocks' and partners believe that an international assignment – or simply a change of climate and environment – will be the answer to their problems. This apparently good idea turns out to be a bad move, however. The strains that inevitably come with any change make the original problem worse. The number of separations and divorces is high in international circles. Often, the liberation felt when living in a foreign country goes hand in hand with liberation from one's partner.

As an executive who worked for many years in Russia described it:

"For men who went without their partners to Russia, I believe very few relationships survived. Most western men have Russian girlfriends, some of them have second families."

The temptation to make a new life with a different partner is high – there are many examples of western managers working in South East Asia who decide to leave their families and marry their Asian girl-friends, for example. And it is not just men who leave their partners or families. There are plenty of cases where the wife or girlfriend decides that the relationship is not going anywhere and enjoys the opportunities that a new country brings.

How can you predict which way your relationship will develop? This is a hot debate among laypeople as well as professional psychol-ogists. Partners change – whereas some aspects of their personality or interests may be predictable, others seem to come out of the blue.

International experience also brings out new facets of a person's personality, as we saw in Chapter 4. This may be a pleasant surprise, but it can also come as a shock: we may start questioning our values or the way we have organized our life and relationships.

Couples often have major problems and crises on their holidays because of heightened expectations of making it a 'special time'. Sim-ilarly, international assignments represent a unique situation in a cou-ple's life together because of the following factors:

▲ The unpredictability of the situation and the potential changes in each partner
▲ Their strong dependence on each other
▲ The absence of a normal social network and support from close friends and family
▲ The lack of normal social controls.

In most cases, it is men who are accompanied abroad by their part-ners. Female international managers do exist, but there are very few of them. For example, in the UK, only 10 percent of managers (and this includes middle to senior management) are female, and only a fraction work internationally. One can therefore safely estimate that at least 95 percent of international managers are men. This situation is bound to change with the stronger career orientation of women in general, the growing numbers of women in management and the increase in women taking MBAs with an international orientation. However, the typical example is still of a working man followed by his partner/spouse.

In most cases, therefore, the female partner has to deal with the challenges of settling into a new place. These include:

▲ Getting the practicalities of the move sorted out.
▲ Finding a way to organize the basics of daily life (schools, shopping, leisure etc.).
▲ Keeping the children happy and making settling in as smooth as possible.
▲ Providing home comforts and support to the husband/partner while he comes to grips with the new job.
▲ Establishing a social network for the children, the husband and herself.

The demands on the 'trailing' partner are plentiful and the support structure is minimal in most cases. There is great pressure on the woman to function to the fullest and 'make it happen'. She has to be an independent, self-reliant and undemanding operator who will pull the strings together in an international move.

The working husband has to adapt to the new environment and often does not have the time to monitor the wife's situation and her feelings during the first few months. He may also miss out on his children's adaptation process. The adjustment can certainly be harder for the partner or the family, as they often have less pre-assignment preparation, are in closer daily contact with the new culture and may therefore experience more intense culture shock. The partner or family is also more starkly confronted with the frustrations of not being able to get things done and, most importantly, they do not have a corporate structure to fall back on.

Annabel Hendry, an anthropologist (currently working in the British Foreign Office) who researched the role of diplomatic wives, points out that in traditional marriages, the wife absorbs the stresses of family life. She makes a convincing argument for how this can affect marital relationships. Absorbing the family's stresses, including the husband's worries, can result in symptoms of depression, similar to those in the culture shock model. As a result, the wife withdraws or shows negative emotions. Often, the reason for this behavior is not clear to the husband, which makes it difficult for him to understand his wife. If the situation is prolonged, he may look for support elsewhere, culminating in serious marital problems.

Are marital problems more likely to occur in particular locations? In Hendry's experience, the traditional hardship places and life on a compound make people more inward looking: "For example, Islamabad has a very bad reputation for generating depression and marital problems."

Frequent flyers

Short-term international work is becoming more and more frequent. Managers like Robert, described in the case below, are firmly rooted in their own country but take on serious international responsibilities. This will not require relocation but will involve traveling abroad for several weeks at a time, sorting things out quickly and learning to understand a new culture at racing speed.

*R*obert *was a businessman firmly rooted in his UK location until the opportunity to develop business in South East Asia came up. He was sent to Singapore in the late 1980s in order to find out whether the company should set up a new venture. With no international experience at all, he took a careful and systematic approach to this venture. He did some research on the country through the* Financial Times *and he also talked to a lot of people who had been out in Singapore.*

He managed to develop the business after an initial three-week orientation stay in Singapore. He met potential partners and also went to see other contacts in order to take references on the potential partners. Subsequently the operation took off and it is probably the success of this operation that got him appointed as chairman of the same company.

Now he goes to Singapore several times a year on short trips to see the operation, develop more business and spend a lot of time entertaining business contacts. He has learned about the Chinese business practice of building relationships outside work, he has clearly seen and enjoyed the importance of karaoke (a 'must' in Asian business entertainment) and he has developed such strong relationships that he was invited to the wedding of his Singaporean MD's son.

Relationship problems can be exacerbated for frequent flyers and in short-term international work. As one international executive reported:

"I was traveling all the time on short-term international assignments. Whereas I myself saw it as an extremely exhilarating experience and loved to travel, my wife in a way 'stayed behind'. She did not have an interest in international issues and we therefore drifted apart."

Short-term assignments can carry high reward and high risk at the same time, as the next examples illustrate.

Evan was an international banker who had worked in France, Germany, Macao, Hong Kong, Portugal, Greece, Poland and Tokyo. He has never actually lived abroad for a longer period but has been on international short-term assignments for the last couple of years. In the mid-1980s, he lived for three months in a hotel, not getting home at all, and he worked practically 24 hours a day.

He loves international work and is happy with the way his outlook has changed. As a consequence, he is now not particularly happy with the lifestyle he has when he is not on a challenging international assignment and he has higher and higher expectations of life. Being on a 'high' and working under conditions which produce strong adrenalin results in a kind of addiction. As he explained, "It is a bit like going back to university when taking exams. There is a very high personal involvement and at the end of it, there is often a depressive phase."

Working on challenging projects with senior executives is certainly professionally important. However, there are costs to someone's personal life in finding a compromise between this demanding type of work and a balanced lifestyle. Evan now finds it very difficult to relax and to switch off as a consequence of his highly pressured international work. Even months after leaving an international assignment, he feels that he still hasn't lost the frantic pace. Possibly as a consequence of his high-pressured international work, he is now separated from his wife and children.

*F*rank *is an American professional who has been working at international level for over 20 years. He has had exposure to doing business in 83 different countries and can be described as a truly international (short-term assignment) professional. He was influenced to move in an international direction by his background – he had many international friends at school and attended a university with a strong international student body.*

He is clearly someone who thrives on new situations, the buzz of international travel ("whizzing first class around the globe and living on champagne and caviar") and learning new things all the time. He enjoys the thrill of meeting new people and is obviously an extremely positive and energetic individual. However, he has also experienced the downside of permanent international travel. His first marriage broke down – by his own account, because his wife was not interested in international issues and she could not empathize with him.

A highly experienced manager gave the following recommendations for dealing with short-term assignments:

*"V*ery *often people do not speak the language of the country and organizations do not even encourage people to learn the language; this is a terrible mistake. People should be forced to take language lessons.*

On the first trip, an international manager should ideally be accompanied by a more senior colleague to take him/her around.

Organizations should also pay more attention to the fact that employees on frequent short-term international travel are very often tired and need some extra time off to reduce the exhaustion. In a way, organizations should give them a bit of special treatment. "

An article in the *Financial Times* (13 January 1997) emphasized the specific stress symptoms associated with frequent short-term international travel. The most obvious are the lack of sleep and disturbed sleeping patterns, but a more serious stress symptom is the inability to associate all the facts to make a decision after the flight. One international manager commented that he never made a significant decision in the first week after a long-haul flight; the implications of this for executives continually flying back and forth across the Atlantic are obvious. Health hazards can be serious for frequent flyers because of their lifestyle and these can include ulcers, heart attacks, psychological problems and breakdowns. Organizations such as the World Bank (where half of the staff are frequent flyers) report higher than average rates of divorces and suicides.

Seasoned international travelers have standard routines to combat the negative effects of flying. For example, while flying do only two things: sleep or work.

Further advice for frequent flyers includes the following:

▲ Always use the same airline, book the same seat number and stay in the same hotel.
▲ Try to extend your stay by at least one day and do something to relax.
▲ Take your partner/spouse on business trips in order to have more time together and to give you support.
▲ To combat jetlag, always adjust to the lifestyle of the country straight away, including its eating and sleeping patterns.
▲ Try to spend as much time as possible outside after arrival – to increase exposure to the sun and the production of melatonin. This helps to adjust your biorhythm to the new timezone.
▲ Cut down on alcohol and drink water throughout the flight.

One frequent flyer reported:

> *"I am fully aware of the physical as well as psychological demands of short-term international travel. One has to be careful to balance it out in order to be efficient when one arrives for an international business meeting. One has to have the personality to adapt to short-term international travel. European*

flights are OK but long-haul flights if one only stays one or two days at the destination are extremely exhausting, often resulting in sleeping disorders and other physical problems. My advice to short-term international travelers is as follows:

▲ *Try to be on top form when going to meetings (both physically as well as psychologically). Get sufficient sleep, and don't work on the plane but relax or do some light reading in order to have full concentration in the meeting.*

▲ *Be careful when you make an exhausting trip. For example, if you make one mid-week, you can feel the exhaustion in the latter part of the week. It may therefore be better to do the trips towards the weekend so that you can relax and are on better form for the next working week.*

▲ *Take light luggage and make the traveling as easy as possible. I usually take a light thriller as well as my CD player with classical music to relax. I also try to do some background reading on the place I am going to and at least buy a travel guide.*

My 'comfort zones' to which I can withdraw abroad or in times of stress are riding and being in the fresh air, as well as having a lot of massages. **"**

An interview with a 'Euro flyer' who commutes between the UK and the continent every week shows the special challenges. This manager gave the following account:

" *I feel I can cope with the demands of being in different places all the time. I have always been able to work strange hours and to juggle a lot of balls in the air, but I can also see that my family needs more reassurance. They find it probably more difficult to cope with my frantic life. In terms of the company, I would have expected more support. They do not realize the effect of short-term international travel, despite being an international company. Ideally, I would expect from my company more flexibility but also more trust. I would expect the company to treat me as a mature individual.*

    What helped me personally to adapt to short-term international work are the following personality characteristics:

independence, self-discipline, cultural sensitivity, being open and light-hearted, being positive, being assertive, and not being arrogant but humble.

My career expectations have completely changed as I now think much more globally. I think nothing of picking up the phone and arranging a meeting in another country or on another continent, whereas before this would have never occurred to me. The only negative effect of my frantic lifestyle is that I have become much more aggressive and less patient and people have in fact commented on this. I do believe I have become less tolerant of people who want to waste time and in such situations my temper has become shorter. On the other hand, I believe I have developed a deeper and better understanding of people.

Another area that I need to guard for my own development is the private life/professional life distinction. Because I have a highly stressful international job, I find it difficult to switch off and therefore my lifestyle has become extremely pacey and adrenalin driven. I now find it quite hard to slow down in my personal life and I want to pack in all the social activities in a very short space of time. There is definitely not enough balance in terms of relaxation in my life. This is obviously a risk in terms of long-term stress but it also puts a certain pressure on my personal relationships. **"**

Does frequent international travel result in an addiction to accumulating air miles? A survey by Global Integration of more than 1000 multinational managers showed that it is quite typical for them to take between four and six foreign trips a month. The effect on their personal life is evident.

Organizations should question whether face-to-face meetings are absolutely necessary. There is an argument that some executives do not use the advances in communication technology as much as they should. In the end, every manager has to strike a fine balance between managing remote teams by modern technology and the necessity to have face-to-face meetings.

Dual careers

In 1993, Shell International conducted a massive survey of its international managers in order to find out what their major concerns were and manage them more effectively. Over 6000 international managers and over 4000 spouses participated. One important aim of the survey was to review the mobility of staff and family and so help the company with better human resource planning.

The survey showed that mobility is highest among younger staff, typically drops off mid-career and then rises again among older staff. Overall, the results suggested that full mobility is declining – a worrying trend for an international company. A higher proportion of staff were fully mobile during the 1980s compared to 1993 and Shell expects that even fewer staff will be fully mobile in the future.

The mobility issue is probably related to the main concerns of the international manager, as illustrated in the same survey:

▲ The spouse – especially in relation to the spouse's career
▲ The children's education – particularly as fewer children are
   going to boarding schools but instead follow their parents abroad.

It is estimated that by the year 2000, 75 percent of international managers will be involved in a dual-career scenario. Either companies will assist partners in finding a suitable job abroad (if the partner does not do this themselves) or the partner will have to take a career break and think of other ways of keeping busy and happy. In our world of old-fashioned stereotypes, it is still assumed that it is easier for women to follow and men to lead in an international career move. This makes it more difficult for married high-flying women to embark on an international career, and may therefore reduce the chances of women succeeding in international management in the long run.

The following case shows the experience of an American executive whose husband followed her to the UK without clear career prospects:

*S*haron is a US business manager who was on her own request transferred to the UK operation of her company. Her husband was, in her description, a '1990s man' who decided to give up his position and have a change in career. They subsequently settled in London but she felt the stresses of being the main wage earner in a new country. Her husband clearly experienced the uniqueness of being a male 'trailing spouse' – he was asked at cocktail parties how it felt being a 'kept man'. After an initial period of struggle, with her husband trying to find a new career and job, they feel settled after four years and enjoy the quality of life in London.

A similar account was given by an HR professional working in Spain:

*M*onica is an HR professional who was sent from her UK base to the Spanish subsidiary of her company. As a linguist with a strong interest in international management, the work in Spain seemed an ideal step in her career progression. Monica and her spouse took the still unusual decision that her husband would give up his full-time job to follow her. In this case, the 'trailing spouse' was a career man who decided to take a sabbatical.

The couple found the experience enlightening. After the typical start-up difficulties, Monica settled down in her job and enjoyed the challenge of working with people who were differently minded. For her husband, things were not quite as easy as anticipated: he enjoyed the job-free period but found himself in a minority role, as all other trailing spouses were female and organized shopping and tea parties in the expatriate spouses network!

Whether it is the exceptional circumstance of men trailing their working wives or the stereotypical example of wives following their husbands, a partner who cannot obtain a work permit or find a suitable job has to put their career on hold. This can be positive if the partner has strong interests outside work or wants to engage in further studies, such as distance learning courses. However, if this is not the case and the three-year sabbatical seriously interrupts a partner's career progression, having a luxury lifestyle, more time to oneself and the opportunity to shop and go to tea parties may not be enough.

Even for partners who do not intend to work, a lack of structure may be difficult to deal with. If you are in an expatriate paradise with all the chores being done for you and the maid looking after the children, your role is diminished and this may be a threat to your identity.

Successful international adaptation depends on whether the accompanying partner is willing to move, can find an equivalent job or will accept the fact that they will not be working while overseas. Within a competitive job market, fewer spouses/partners are willing to take a career break and trail overseas. As working spouses are becoming much more the rule than the exception, both international managers and companies should ideally address this issue early on. Although career breaks and diversification are becoming much more acceptable, a succession of gaps in a CV still raises doubts in any prospective employer about the individual's career motivation.

Possibly as a result of its 1993 survey, Shell International has taken positive action and created a service for its families in an enterprise called OUTPOST. Although not directly a career-counseling service for the spouse, OUTPOST is family oriented and provides information on expatriate locations (including videos and CDs about the life of international managers, magazines and newsletters by other international managers in Shell locations around the world and information for children). The center recommends schools and medical services and provides information on employment opportunities in the widest sense (including self-employment and voluntary work). Shell International is also progressive in that it financially supports any training that a spouse undertakes during an assignment overseas. Similar financial aid is offered by Motorola (*Financial Times*, 6 May 1998). As part of the service at Shell, there is also an expatriate transfer adviser, a spouse employment consultant and an education adviser, all based in The Hague (Netherlands).

Unfortunately, not every spouse enjoys the benefits of a supportive organization, as the following case study shows:

Shelley was a highly qualified management consultant who was trained in the USA and worked at an international management school in Asia. She decided to give up her position and move with her husband to the UK, after his organization promised to help her find a position there. On arrival, she discovered difficulties in finding an appropriate position. The organization did not provide the support she expected and her job search was hindered as organizations were not able to assess her competence in an objective way and complained that she didn't have connections within the country or a UK education. Even in a highly international city such as London, many organizations do not think internationally.

Ideally, the working partner should carry out an evaluation of career goals, abilities, interests, ambitions and potential job avenues. It may also be worth considering more formal career advice and counseling. This could take the following form:

▲ An interview with a career expert, assessing professional experience, career history and technical skills.
▲ A psychological assessment, focusing on personality, interests, abilities, motivation and adaptability.
▲ Integrating the information with regard to job opportunities in the country concerned and specific conditions regarding work permits, regulations, accreditation of professional qualifications, etc.

The result of this exercise would be the development of an action plan that is compatible with career aspirations, skills, personality and the employment conditions of the particular country. Even if the company or the individual does not want to spend the money required for formal and comprehensive expert advice, the spouse could still take some basic steps in this direction.

In international cities such as London, Brussels, The Hague, Geneva or Paris, women have been proactive in setting up counseling services on a voluntary basis. For example, Focus Information Services in London is a non-profit resource center for international residents, entirely run by voluntary staff of expatriate wives. The Focus Newsletter includes job advertisements as well as networking events. Focus is sponsored by US multinationals such as AT&T and General Electric and organizes seminars on career-related issues, including interviewing techniques, CV writing and cultural briefings. There is a partner organization in Brussels.

Checklist for working partners

▲ Is the spouse's current job directly transferable to the new country?

▲ Are their qualifications recognized in the country concerned?

▲ Does the spouse need a work permit and how difficult is this to organize?

▲ Will the partner's company help to organize a work permit and sponsor it?

▲ Are there arrangements by the organization to find a job for the spouse/partner or reciprocal arrangements with other multinational companies?

▲ If the previous career cannot be continued in the new country, what will make for an interesting, enjoyable and useful career break? (See Chapter 7 on career planning.)

▲ What activities did the spouse/partner always want to try and could see as an alternative to their present career?

▲ Are there any particular courses that the spouse/partner could do in the country or by distance learning?

▲ Does the spouse/partner know the language of the country or do they want to learn it or improve their grasp?

▲ Could cultural study of the new country represent a full-time pursuit? What are possible voluntary activities?

▲ What organizations are available in the country for working partners? These may include those established by particular nationalities (such as Focus, founded by US expatriates) or by multinational corporations (such as OUTPOST).

▲ What information can be gained through your country's embassy and what networking activities can be established either through the embassy or through bilateral Chambers of Commerce?

Universally adaptable children?

It is generally assumed that children will find it easy to adapt (easier than adults, at any rate) and that parents should not expect them to experience too many difficulties. It is true that children are often surprisingly adaptable and take new situations, however alien, in their stride. Nevertheless, just as their parents will have different levels of adaptability, so children have their own personalities and characteristics that will either help them cope with change or make it difficult.

Some children simply need a lot of stability and security. These children will not adapt easily to an international move, as the following case shows:

Joanna was the youngest daughter of an internationally mobile family. Her father was an executive who moved around the world throughout his career. As a consequence, her mother had to give up her own career and follow him wherever he went, which was a continual source of frustration. From an early age, Joanna reacted very badly to any move – she would get a high fever, dizziness and be generally sick. She had always felt insecure and developed psychological problems later on.

As a result, her father decided against taking on further foreign assignments for a while and the family opted for an extended stay in their home country. Her psychological symptoms were identified as part of a family problem – particularly related to her mother's career frustration.

Not all examples are as extreme. The next shows a different area of which parents should be aware:

James was the son of an executive who was posted to South East Asia. Both his father and his mother worked and his mother managed to find an interesting position. Despite his parents' happy situation, James did not adapt well in the new location. He was not happy with the school, he had too many changes of school and he

> *also was the only British child in the school. He became somewhat withdrawn and unhappy.*
>
> *Partly as a consequence, the parents decided not to extend their four-year contract but to come back to the UK. There, James started to blossom. He now really enjoys the school and his life in a more stable environment.*

Traditionally, children of expatriates were sent to boarding school. However, parents nowadays are more reluctant to send their children to a school thousands of miles away. They want to be involved in their children's development and education and are keen for the children to accompany them to the new country, as the results of the Shell survey showed.

This pattern has also been supported by other surveys. ECA's 1996 mobility survey of a large number of international companies showed that the two most common reasons for someone turning down an international assignment were the partner's career and concerns about children.

Not being able to have primary and secondary school education for their children in their own language in the host country will restrict employees' international mobility. But apart from the availability of good schools in the host country, it is also important to be sensitive to children's social and emotional development. Depending on the child's developmental stage and personality, a stint abroad can be highly conducive to development or something of a nightmare. Preschool children often adapt fast, playing with other children even if they do not share a common language and learning foreign languages surprisingly fast. Five-year-olds who come out of Chinese-speaking primary schools with an astonishing grasp of Mandarin are not a rare case – to the frustration of their non-Mandarin-speaking parents.

For older children, belonging to a group becomes more and more important and the availability of a peer group with which they can identify is essential. This may be an international group or one of the same nationality. It is difficult for children to be in a minority, with no other minorities around, as the example of James illustrates.

Having a highly privileged lifestyle also leads to some children being spoilt and, in extreme cases, becoming disrespectful or even racist in relation to host nationals. There may be a loss of perspective because there is no feeling of belonging or sense of social responsibility. Children could end up lacking clear values and norms of what is right and wrong because they do not have a consistent social framework.

In a survey by Wilkinson (1989) about families' reactions to the news of an assignment in Malaysia, only 38 percent of children really looked forward to it, 37 percent were indifferent and 25 percent preferred not to go. Children are often not as positive as the rest of the family when it comes to going abroad. The most positive is usually the manager taking the assignment, as in Wilkinson's study.

Ideally, parents should give their children detailed descriptions of the country and the lifestyle in order for them to develop a positive attitude towards the move. Alston and Stratford (1996) showed that parental behavior, particularly changes in that behavior when relocating, is the strongest predictor of children's anxiety in an international move. This makes sense, as parents' stresses have an impact on their children's emotional state.

ECA, an international consultancy with headquarters in London, has developed a systems-based questionnaire to help prospective international managers and their families weigh up the pros and cons of moving abroad. This encourages them to reflect carefully on the implications of a move and prevents an impulsive approach to decision making.

Practical advice: the relocation checklist

International managers sometimes take some unusual items overseas. Items transported have included swings, hamsters, goldfish, the contents of a wine cellar and a dead body.

It seems sensible to have a comprehensive relocation checklist that gives managers clear guidelines about what to do at what time. Relocation companies produce detailed checklists, such as the one suggested by HCR World Connect and detailed below.

Pre-departure

Assignment initiation
▲ Contact relocation adviser to determine allowances, etc.
▲ Get timescales agreed.
▲ Decide whether to rent or sell house.
▲ Place house on market if necessary.
▲ Decide whether to take or sell car.
▲ Research destination.
▲ Arrange area tour and select property.
▲ Consider education arrangements.
▲ Discuss quarantine requirements for pets.
▲ Apply for visas and work permits.
▲ Check passports are valid.
▲ Consult tax adviser.
▲ Consider working partner support.

One month before
▲ Hold car boot/garage sale.
▲ Get medical, dental and school records (or copies).
▲ Arrange travel insurance.
▲ Clear any outstanding debts and taxes.
▲ Send change of address cards.
▲ Arrange for mail to be redirected.
▲ Finalize travel plans.
▲ Make hotel reservations.
▲ Check electrical appliances for compatibility.
▲ Arrange shipment of any high-value goods.
▲ Have relevant vaccinations.
▲ Start language/intercultural training.
▲ Complete area tour and school selection.
▲ Arrange tenancy management (if renting house).

Two weeks before
▲ Collect dry cleaning and anything sent for repair.
▲ Return borrowed items, e.g. videos, library books.
▲ Give unwanted items to charity.
▲ Arrange transfer of bank accounts.

▲ Cancel/transfer magazine subscriptions.
▲ Cancel cable/satellite accounts.
▲ Arrange for utility readings on day of move.

One week before
▲ Sort airfreight – keep on one side.
▲ Put passports, tickets etc. in safe place.
▲ Select games and books for journey.
▲ Empty and defrost fridge/freezer (at least 48 hours before move).
▲ Bring laundry up to date.
▲ Cancel newspapers and milk.

One day before
▲ Pack accompanied baggage.

On the day

▲ Keep calm!
▲ Hand keys to estate agent if required.

At destination

▲ Arrange for freight to clear customs and be delivered (note that any insurance claims may have a time limit attached).
▲ Register as required with police, councils etc.
▲ Arrange acclimatization days.
▲ Change driving license or take test if necessary.
▲ Buy TV license, if required.
▲ Register and insure car.
▲ Arrange working partner support.

Relocation companies have extended their services from transporting possessions to something that is much more comprehensive. They can offer the following types of services:

▲ Work permits, visas and renewals
▲ Pre-departure intercultural orientation and foreign language training
▲ International transportation service
▲ International property management
▲ International home sales
▲ Educational assistance
▲ Repatriation program.

Housing and education

Relocation companies and information systems on international assignments, such as Employment Conditions Abroad (ECA) in London and the ORC (Organization Resources Counselers) in the USA, will be able to provide general information on housing availability and the quality of housing (comparability with housing standards in your own country).

For example, it is useful to have information such as that shown in Table 11 for cities in eastern Europe, based on data compiled by international companies.

Table 11 Housing availability in eastern Europe

City	Housing availability
Moscow	Difficult
	Expatriate housing is expensive
Prague	Very scarce and expensive
Warsaw	Improving
Sofia	Reasonable housing
	Relatively expensive

Similar information can be gained in relation to international schooling (Table 12).

Table 12 Availability of international schooling in eastern Europe

City	Schooling availability
Moscow	Good foreign schools but with long waiting lists
Prague	Good international school but places are scarce
Warsaw	Long waiting lists for western schools
Sofia	Only one school – no waiting list

Medical issues in tropical countries

Working in tropical countries requires some special preparation in medical terms before departure.

Medical examination

This examination should ideally be carried out by a medical doctor who is trained in tropical medicine. Addresses of specialists can easily be obtained through central health services. Apart from a general assessment of medical fitness for living in a tropical country, the medical specialist should concentrate in the consultation on the personal life and professional situation of the international manager as well as the situation of the family.

An important criterion for 'tropical fitness' is the exclusion of a chronic illness (such as heart disease, diabetes, chronic eye disease, renal disease) – all of these can carry significant risks in a tropical climate. Moreover, if the international manager has suffered a previous psychological illness such as depression or psychosis (even if this has only appeared once), their current psychological state should be thoroughly assessed. The stress of moving abroad could bring on a new outbreak of the illness; particularly if there are no adequate support structures available, this could have serious consequences.

Immunizations and inoculations

You should contact a medical specialist as early as possible to plan an inoculation program specifically tailored to your destination. Sufficient time should be allowed between individual inoculations and the inoculation program should be completed about 10 days before traveling.

Information about inoculations and medical recommendations is published annually by the World Health Organisation (WHO) in a brochure called *International Travel and Health*.

Other considerations

Apart from the general risks in some tropical countries (such as the prevalence of specific diseases), one also has to consider the exact location: will the manager and family be living in a big city or in the countryside? What are the hygiene conditions? Does the working environment bring any particular stresses? In countries with endemic diseases, the specialist will suggest the precautions to be taken.

In many Asian and Latin American cities, the medical support is comparable to western standards. However, in some African capitals no adequate medical support is available. Before departing from your home country, the exact medical infrastructure of the host country should be thoroughly investigated. Your company should ideally give specific information on addresses of medical specialists and hospitals in the host country.

Special issues with children

Newborn babies should not travel to tropical countries before they are six to eight weeks old and then only if the living conditions of the family abroad are defined and predictable. Medically, the adaptation of healthy older babies as well as smaller children up to primary school age is generally unproblematic. With older children and teenagers, there is often a question whether the conditions of the country match their individual and social interests. Moreover, it is often not easy for

European teenagers to adapt to life in a developing country. Frequent changes of location make it difficult for children to learn how to develop and maintain friends, which could cause problems later.

A thorough pediatric assessment should be planned early on. If the child has a chronic disease, a stay in the tropics is only possible if the treatment can be carried out by parents or if there is a specialist nearby.

Practical recommendations for preventing disease

▲ Water: be sure to have clean drinking water. Use filters or treat water with chlorine or similar chemicals.
▲ Living conditions (particularly important for families):
   — Put mosquito grills around windows
   — Use mosquito nets over beds
   — Eliminate stagnant water around the house (this is a breeding ground for insects).
▲ Particularly in rural areas, the infrastructure and availability of a range of foods should be checked.
▲ Be careful with your eating habits and eat a lot of fruit and vegetables. Be careful with alcohol.
▲ Do sports as well as ensuring that you have sufficient sleep.
▲ Only engage in safe sex. AIDS and other sexually transmitted diseases are a particular risk in some countries, exacerbated by the promiscuous behavior of some expatriates.
▲ Try to get additional health insurance that will cover the treatment of all potential diseases in the foreign country but also guarantees transfer home if necessary.
▲ Psychological stress, particularly at the beginning of international work, can contribute to a higher risk of developing diseases.
▲ Spend time in stocking up your 'home pharmacy' – ideally get medical advice on this.

Coming home – the biggest culture shock of all?

Most managers believe that returning to your own country is simplicity itself. Once they have settled the practicalities of moving their family and sorting out somewhere to live, they expect to fall back into their usual routine. They look forward to seeing their friends and family again and to enjoying the special treats their home country has to offer.

'Coming home' is unfortunately not that simple for many returning international managers. Their own country has changed, their organization has changed, their friends and family may have changed and, most importantly, they themselves have changed. These factors could make the return home the biggest culture shock of all, often called reverse culture shock.

The returning manager and their family will have to deal with two main issues: personal readaptation and professional reintegration. We will focus here on the process of personal readaptation and look at professional reintegration in Chapter 7.

Personal readaptation

Many returnees go through similar phases of adaptation to when they went abroad, such as:

▲ Initial euphoria – the honeymoon feeling of being back, seeing familiar faces and eating familiar food.
▲ Irritability and alienation – the realization that things have changed, not being up to date with new products, methods, ways of approaching things.
▲ Gradual adjustment – social reintegration, modification of former lifestyle to match 'new' interests.
▲ Breaking through – feeling content and adjusted again.

Expecting to fall back into your familiar environment and realizing that you have changed are probably the main factors contributing to the feeling of alienation. It comes as a great shock to most people that they are not quite as they were before and that their friends and family cannot really understand their experiences and what they are talking about. Again, you have to think carefully about how you can best integrate your international experience into life at home. It is often useful to talk to others who have gone through the same experience to find out what helped them readapt. This will alleviate the feeling of alienation and disorientation. It may also help to extend your own social circle to include people who have had similar experiences, to try to make friends of different nationalities and, ultimately, to have a more diverse social circle than before.

Alan had some extremely difficult decisions to make at repatriation stage. He had lived in the Far East for several years and had just come back to the UK. According to his own description, he had become depressed months before because he did not want to return to Britain. In Japan, he lived apart from his family and he obviously enjoyed the independence. When he returned to Britain, he had to face several dilemmas: first, at a personal level, he was not sure whether he wanted to go back and live with his wife and family. Secondly, he was uncertain whether he would be able to reenter the social network. Thirdly, he did not know what type of job he would be able to get, as his company could not offer him a suitable position at the time.

These kinds of concerns are also reflected in some of the comments in my survey of international managers, in which 25 percent of those interviewed reported difficulties on repatriation. These occurred because of:

▲ Loss of lifestyle
▲ No appropriate job available
▲ Loss of autonomy
▲ Being made redundant
▲ Handling politics at head office
▲ Having to deal with uncertainty on return.

A few managers even considered repatriation as the main problem with a foreign assignment. Several left the company within weeks of coming home, even though they were offered jobs. Nick Forster (1993) described the following problem areas for returnees: 37 percent reported difficulties at work created by reduced work status, 32 percent experienced downward career moves and 38 percent complained of loss of autonomy.

Managers frequently get slotted into jobs on return that are at too low a level and they consequently experience immense frustration. Companies can no longer guarantee jobs for life, but even if a job is guaranteed, sometimes no appropriate position is available.

The following situations frequently occur for returning international managers, illustrated with comments from the managers in my survey.

Unrealistic perception of own country

Long-term expatriates particularly can feel out of sync with developments in their own country. They expect a home country that has not changed in terms of practical aspects as well as general values. Often, our home country is idealized during an international assignment. Especially during stressful times, we start idealizing our own country where 'things are better'. This results in our being disillusioned on return.

"When I came back to the UK, I felt alienated. I was unsettled for at least a year. I felt that I did not fit in. "

"I had problems coming back from Vietnam, adjusting to the lifestyle in the UK. I had autonomy there and coming back, I lost it. Also, I found the culture and the mentality in Asia very different. The attitude in Europe seemed 'poor' in comparison. By poor, I mean that the attitudes in Europe are so negative, compared to the optimism in Vietnam. "

Lack of excitement on return

Being a foreigner certainly has advantages. First of all, you do not feel the strict social control you experience in your own country. This allows more freedom. More importantly, there is an excitement about learning new things every day. Coming home, even if that home has changed, cannot compete with this type of excitement. Boredom sets in and you experience a lack of interest in life in general.

Social isolation

Telling your stories to people who have never lived abroad could make you really depressed. People who do not have a similar international orientation do not want to hear every detail of your foreign adventure. As a consequence, you feel misunderstood and neglected, as you feel other people aren't giving you sufficient attention. More importantly, former friends treat you as if you have not changed at all. If you feel you have changed, this can be a very stifling experience.

> *"My wife was suffering a bit more as she had a good expatriate lifestyle and was part of an expatriate community. Now she spends more time on her own and she misses the lifestyle in Japan. Our lifestyle has definitely downgraded. Whereas in Japan we would always meet people over dinners in restaurants, it is now down to the pub for a couple of pints. In Japan, people I socialized with were all of fairly similar backgrounds (i.e. people who had the same amount of money). In London, my set of friends is of a much more varied nature. "*

Restlessness

Having become used to the challenges of an international assignment, you may continually feel restless on your return.

"I realized that the moving around makes a person very unsettled – you leave a part of you wherever you are and you always miss certain aspects; it certainly makes you less settled."

Five steps to an easy personal reentry

▲ Expect possible symptoms of reverse culture shock (feeling alienated, ill at ease or slightly depressed) and accept that they are normal.

▲ Give yourself time to deal with the changes involved in coming back and deal with the immediate stress (see the stress-reduction advice in Chapter 2).

▲ Use your social support system effectively – in particular, talk to people who have had international experience themselves.

▲ Accept that your interests and expectations have changed – try to expand your previous lifestyle and get more diversity in your activities.

▲ Broaden your social network and try to befriend people of different nationalities.

7

Managing Your Career Successfully

The increase in international positions is evident if you look at the job advertisements in national papers. Attractive international positions certainly catch the eye. However, in order to be successful internationally, it is not sufficient to have all the characteristics of a highly

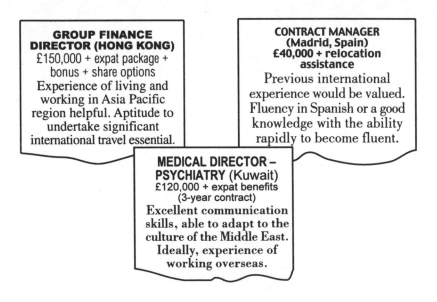

GROUP FINANCE DIRECTOR (HONG KONG)
£150,000 + expat package + bonus + share options
Experience of living and working in Asia Pacific region helpful. Aptitude to undertake significant international travel essential.

CONTRACT MANAGER (Madrid, Spain)
£40,000 + relocation assistance
Previous international experience would be valued. Fluency in Spanish or a good knowledge with the ability rapidly to become fluent.

MEDICAL DIRECTOR – PSYCHIATRY (Kuwait)
£120,000 + expat benefits (3-year contract)
Excellent communication skills, able to adapt to the culture of the Middle East. Ideally, experience of working overseas.

successful international executive. It is also necessary to plan your international career and to use your organization effectively.

This chapter puts international work into the context of career management. First, let's take another look at the effect of international work on personality and career development.

How international work affects your life

Little is known about how international work really affects a manager's life, so I interviewed 45 executives operating internationally to find out about the effects of international work on personality and careers (Marx, 1996a).

Effects on personality

Significant positive effects on their personality were reported by 91 percent of the managers interviewed, as summarized in Table 13. The main effects were greater confidence, more open-mindedness, more tolerance and patience and a broader outlook.

A few of the executives interviewed described negative effects on their personality, such as being less patient, more serious, more cynical, more dogmatic and feeling unsettled.

These potential effects can be illustrated by comments from the managers interviewed:

> *"It made me tougher. I am more capable of taking rapid action and I can cut the problem much earlier on. I followed the advice of 'if it doesn't kill you, it makes you stronger'."*

> *"I grew up, it broadened my horizons and I developed a need for travel and a thirst for knowledge. I felt more flexible and self-sufficient. At the beginning, I was more reserved, but after I adapted, I became more outgoing."*

Table 13 Positive effects on personality

Greater confidence
More open-mindedness, broader outlook
More tolerance and patience
Better listening ability
Greater sensitivity to other cultures
Faster decision making
More maturity
Better understanding of people
Higher degree of independence
More assertiveness
Greater thirst for knowledge
Greater diplomacy and tactfulness
Greater flexibility
Better people management

"I feel more confident overall: I have a broader outlook on things. I feel that if you can deal with stressful situations in a foreign country, this will boost your belief in coping with any difficult situation, like 'if I can do this, I can cope with anything'. The whole experience also brought me closer to my partner and we decided to get married while we were out there. "

"It was a toughening experience – it strengthened my confidence because it is not easy to go to a foreign country and to make it work, to build up business contacts. In the end, I got the praise for my work. "

"One effect the experience had is that I could never take the 'game' seriously afterwards because of all the problems I experienced in Japan. Before, I was completely career motivated but after that, I had different life expectations and I was trying to get my life together. "

It is great to see how positive these international managers (of various nationalities and working in different parts of the world) were about the effect of international work on their personal development. The majority reported great benefits in terms of their personality.

The situation is slightly different when looking at the effects on professional development.

Effects on career

Positive effects of international work on their professional development were reported by 82 percent of the managers interviewed, while 29 percent reported negative effects and some reported a combination of the two.

Positive and negative career effects are detailed in Tables 14 and 15.

Table 14 Positive career effects

General career progression/promotion
Faster professional development
More responsibility/autonomy/senior roles
More marketable

Improvement of specific abilities
Cross-cultural management/international skills
Strategic thinking/negotiation/flexibility
Professional expertise and confidence improved
More politically astute and able to deal with headquarters

Other issues
Career change
More money
More interesting time

Table 15 Negative career effects

International experience not appreciated
Lower-level position on repatriation
Company did not manage to keep them
Zero benefit
International experience discredited
Lost all home-country contacts
Professional progress slower than in home country

Other effects
Being now in a more risky (specialist) area
More power driven
Being away from new ideas and developments
Psychologically very tired after the assignment (lack of energy)

Examples of individual managers' experiences include the following.

"Very good because I went to a country where the industry was not as advanced and, therefore, I could have faster career progression."

"I became more confident. I also developed a broader expertise in transactions. Interestingly, most people who went on secondment at the same time left the company after coming back. Even the hot shots and people who were earmarked for a fast-track career often changed company. It was the opportunity to step back from the treadmill that often led to a change in job."

"I learned a lot about dealing with headquarters and the experience in the United States was a major stepping stone in my career. I feel that international experience is a little like doing an MBA: you cannot pinpoint a particular bit that was useful, but overall it is very useful."

"It has been a bit of a struggle really. I thought the business wasn't going anywhere and it was time to go back. I did not see that there were sufficient opportunities long term."

"I used to think that international experience looked good on your CV, that it is an enhancement, but I am not so sure any more – a lot of people want to see stability but if you have moved around too much, they cannot take that seriously."

"Of all the expatriates that came back from abroad, only one was staying with the company. The company did not know what to do with the international experience of their managers and, therefore, people were underused. I am now going to a much more internationally oriented company. Therefore, my experience has not helped me to progress in my own company but has made me much more marketable outside."

"My training before I went to Paris cost £300,000. I improved the Paris performance by three times and was clearly seen as a high flyer within my company. Nevertheless, my company did not manage to keep me and find me an appropriate job after the assignment."

"I found that my experience in Japan was not really appreciated at all when I came back to London. Sometimes I seriously question whether it was the best thing for me to do because I was marked for a fast-track career to a senior level in London before I left, but then I blew all my contacts and it was difficult to get back."

Seasoned executives

An interview with David John, chairman of BOC, one of the UK's largest companies, will illustrate some of the characteristic personal and professional experiences through which many executives will go during their international careers.

Career background

David John developed the idea of an international career early on when he left Cambridge University to attend graduate school at

Columbia University, New York. He subsequently joined RTZ in London in 1966, then moved to Redland, with assignments in Hong Kong and the Middle East. He worked in Bahrain from 1978 to 1980, then returned to the UK as managing director of a Redland division. He subsequently spent another five years in the Middle East. From March 1987 to 1992, he was based in Singapore.

His international jobs were at senior management level throughout and involved many negotiations in relation to joint projects.

His motivation for taking on the first assignment is interesting. It was at a time of high inflation in the UK and he was worried about his children's private school fees. He was thinking about leaving his company, but then the company offered him a position overseas. The main attraction was the opportunity to start up a new operation in a new country; money was a secondary feature. He went first to Hong Kong and learned about the Chinese culture, before moving to the Middle East and working in Bahrain. He found the culture of the Middle East extremely complex.

Family perspective

The children's education caused some problems. In Hong Kong, there were no difficulties because the schools were good. In the Middle East there was more of a problem finding international schools and the children had to be sent to boarding school. At first, John did not want to send his children away because of his own experience at boarding school. However, in the end, he found it worked very well.

The family took frequent trips together. His wife would often come home to the UK for the summer term and then in the holidays take the children to wherever he was working. They would always make sure that they had a family holiday together, and that they were home for Christmas. John believes that international work puts a high strain on relationships and that a marriage has to be strong to survive; he comments that partners have to be 'flexible, wise and good listeners'.

Adaptation and cross-cultural management

According to John, overseas experience has taught him patience: "Coming with a western attitude of result orientation and swift action doesn't get you very far. You have to learn how to play their way." In terms of management, one of the biggest mistakes he made was while managing Indian employees in the Middle East. The employees were accustomed to a hierarchical way of management – quite a military approach. When he arrived in his job, he abolished all these regimented forms of management but found that this did not work at all, because the Indian employees saw him as a 'soft touch'. Ultimately, he had to adopt a directive and hierarchical management style and show his toughness in order to survive.

Another mistake he made in the Middle East was in Bahrain. Fifteen years ago, he was involved in building a marina club complex. The club was extremely smart and had a huge marble staircase leading up from the entrance hall and then facing a wall. In order to make the space more decorative, John suggested two antique Arabic-style doors in this space. The Arab chairman of the operation rejected this idea outright. The doors reminded him of ancient housing in the desert and not of the modern society they had built in Bahrain. To reflect their modernism, the Bahrainian executives wanted to have glitz and no reminders of their past.

This is a good example of not seeing ideas from your counterparts' perspective and failing to consider the development of the society at the time. Interestingly, the situation has changed: there is now a museum in Bahrain to preserve all the ancient traditions.

John estimates that the percentage of managers who perform well internationally is about 70 percent, leaving the remaining 30 percent struggling with their assignments.

Young high flyers

The following case illustrates how the younger generation of executives structure their careers and the difficulties they typically encounter in career progression. The criterion for a high flyer is an executive who has performed successfully in several international assignments and has an international career. To give some gender balance, this example concerns the career of a female executive in financial services.

Career structure

Although she originally planned to embark on an academic career in political sciences, Caroline Kuhnert decided to move into the business area and joined a trainee program with an Austrian bank in her native Vienna. For two years she worked in the city in a relatively junior position, being trained and gaining general banking experience.

Because of her academic specialization in political science in Russia and her language skills, she decided to apply for a position in Moscow. By her own account, she was extremely fortunate because the bank had failed to fill the position in Moscow for two years before she came along. She jumped about two steps in her career and obtained a fairly senior position as head of representative office at a relatively young age. She stayed for three years in this position and was offered the opportunity to move into senior management of the International Bank of Moscow, of which her bank was a co-owner. She stayed two years with this bank.

Kuhnert planned her next career step quite carefully. She accepted a position with Creditanstalt in London which was less senior and accepted a cut in her salary in order to expand her banking skills. She stayed two years in this position – and then again decided to make a drastic change and go into investment banking for similar reasons: she wanted to learn about different areas in financial services.

Kuhnert sees her career progression as a combination of planning and good luck. Objectively, her planning seems shrewd and intelligent, with an excellent sense of timing. Her ambition is to learn as much as possible about all areas of banking and thus be perfectly prepared for a board position in 10 years' time. However, she also recognizes the potential risk of burnout that long working hours, performance pressure and frequent international travel can bring. Kuhnert made a switch from two longer-term assignments in Russia to being based in London with frequent, short-term international travel, mostly to various regions within Russia.

Curriculum Vitae

Name: Caroline Kuhnert
Nationality: Austrian
Current Position: Executive Director in Debt Capital Markets at SBC Warburg Dillon Read (London)
Academic Background: PhD in Political Science (University of Vienna)
MA in Political Science (University of Vienna)
Study periods in Paris and Moscow
Languages: German, Russian, English, French, Italian

Career History:

1997 to date	*UBS and subsequently SBC Warburg Dillon Read, London* Executive Director in Debt Capital Markets
1995–1997	*Creditanstalt, London* Head of Structured Trade Finance Assistant Director
1994–1996	*International Moscow Bank, Moscow* General Manager International Customer Division
1991–1994	*Creditanstalt, Moscow* Head of Representative Office
1989–1991	*Girozentrale und Bank der Oesterreichischen Sparkassen AG, Vienna* International Project Finance Department

Kuhnert's advice for international managers is to keep their focus on career planning. The challenge is to keep a balance in the relationship with headquarters and to be sure that you perform well, but also to publicise that fact. Your PR skills in an international assignment are as important as your knowledge and performance.

This is consistent with stories of international managers who stay abroad for a long time, do not spend enough effort liaising with headquarters and ensuring they know the decision makers. They often mismanage their careers and do not achieve the career progression they deserve. For anyone who is recruited externally, i.e. is new to a company, it is important to spend sufficient time in headquarters before going on the foreign assignment. This will ensure enough knowledge of the company, the decision makers and the organizational politics. Otherwise, it is virtually impossible to represent the company abroad or to influence headquarters.

Kuhnert's career is interesting as it shows an unusual range of experience and a varied background. Her CV and career progression lead to the following evaluation:

▲ An unusual background in political sciences before moving into banking shows a good range of interests and flexible skills.
▲ Early international orientation with many stays abroad as a student as well as strong language skills.
▲ Early international moves into a position in Vienna at a relatively junior level.
▲ A smart career move into a senior position at International Moscow Bank, being confronted by a team of much older, male team members. This also allowed her to make two jumps on the career ladder. A good but high-risk strategy.
▲ After Moscow, the ability to forgo some of her salary in order to take up a position in a new field and a different country.
▲ The CV suggests strong career progression, with good moves in terms of her long-term career potential.

First timers

Deborah Percy is a British HR professional working with Blockbuster, a video rental company. She was promoted to vice-president, international human resources, based in Dallas. This new role expanded her original operation in nine countries to 26 countries. She described her adaptation in personal and professional terms:

    66 *Ideally I would have liked to stay a bit longer in my European HR role before moving to the USA. However, since this opportunity came up and it was an excellent promotion I had to take it.*

      Basically, I can differentiate two main phases in terms of adaptation. The first three weeks were full of curiosity and dealing with the practicalities and went OK, but also had their ups and

downs in terms of frustrations, such as banking etc. Thereafter, I started to look around and to ask the necessary questions and to learn to develop. I think the recipe is not to make assumptions about the other culture, in my case about the Americans, and not to assume anything really. This leaves you open to ask many questions and to become more self-aware as to how you come across.
My adaptation went well altogether. "

Probably one sign of her positive adaptation after 12 months in the USA, her first international assignment, is the fact that she has now decided to stay there because she finds it a much more balanced lifestyle. She has more time for herself and outside work activities.

She gives this advice for managing an international career:

▲ Try to find a mentor in the first three weeks.
▲ Do some cultural orientation before you go to the country and after a period there.
▲ Identify all your assumptions and check them out before you go.
▲ Avoid your partner/spouse coming to join you six months later – this is too long. You may be out of sync in your adaptation.
▲ Do not sell your home, as it is good to leave a base.
▲ Expect to deal with culture shock for about six months at least.

"*After 12 months, I am still trying to understand; the international experience has made me more curious about my own culture and mentality.* "

A new career pattern

Traditionally, high flyers joined large (preferably multinational) companies, started in the graduate scheme and followed a career that was set out by the company. Fast and consistent promotion within the same company was their career aim and the company did its best to retain them. This pattern has changed dramatically over the last couple of years.

The younger generation of top executives have a different background. An analysis of the career profiles of chief executives of the top

100 companies in the UK (Marx, 1996c) showed that a completely new generation of chief executives is emerging. Compared to the older generation, these executives:

▲ are better educated (they are more likely to have university degrees)
▲ often have advanced degrees
▲ are more likely to have international experience
▲ have worked for a larger number of companies, i.e. changed companies more often.

The young generation of chief executives structure their career differently: they take more risks, they seek diversity and they don't follow the traditional path of staying for a long time with the same company. They seek new challenges, including international assignments.

This pattern is encouraging for international managers. First, it suggests that international experience is valued. Secondly, it means that taking risks and joining different types of company may pay dividends in the long run and result in better jobs. Risk taking and diversification reflect an ability to adapt to different environments and to be flexible – characteristics that are important for success in today's complex and fast-changing business environment. Lateral career moves and experience with different types of industry are certainly encouraged and seen as much more positive than in the past.

Another consideration is the effect of international experience on salaries. I recently tried to find out what differentiated executives (of the same age) who had a high salary from those who had a lower salary. I focused on a group of finance directors applying for positions in the UK. Compared to those earning lower salaries, senior finance professionals with high salaries were:

▲ nearly three times as likely to have had international experience, defined as an overseas assignment (45 versus 16 percent)
▲ more likely to work in the finance sector (35 versus 24 percent)
▲ more likely to have a directorship (85 versus 72 percent).

The aim of the survey was to find pointers on how to achieve higher salaries. If you want to make money as a finance professional, the advice is: get international experience, work in the finance sector and get a directorship. International experience was the most significant factor distinguishing the two groups.

In a report on *Building and Retaining Global Talent: Towards 2002*, Johnson (1998) explained:

> *There will be a major change in international business operations as old style expatriate policies and procedures are becoming out of date. Even more important, old style expatriates are becoming out of date too.*

We have seen throughout this book that international managers come in many shapes, beyond the traditional expatriate: there are shorter-term assignments, project work, virtual international teams and so on. Johnson's research on 150 organizations worldwide identifies the following new types:

▲ Solo managers on short-term assignments (without families)
▲ Solo managers on long-term assignments (without families)
▲ 'In-betweenies' whose spouses will go if the company will find a job for them
▲ Female executives with trailing husbands
▲ The over-fifties who are willing to travel (leaving their grown-up children behind).

International development

Barham and Oates (1993) suggest the following steps to prepare for an international career:

Expand your global thinking and expertise
▲ Read international newspapers and magazines on a consistent basis (*Economist, Financial Times, International Herald Tribune*)
▲ Read the latest publications on how to do international business
▲ Read international trade journals to keep up with international developments in your field.

Establish global links and networks
▲ Develop formal and informal cross-border networks in your own company
▲ Join international associations in your functional expertise
▲ Try to attend as many international conferences as you can.

Develop global leadership and values
▲ Learn about cross-cultural management and the management of international teams
▲ Know your own values and behavior and the impact you create on other people
▲ Learn different languages.

For up-to-date information on specific countries, a new online survival guide for international managers, Countrynet, has been launched by Arthur Andersen, the Economist Intelligence Unit and Craighead Publications. It is a subscription-based Website with information on 84 countries on issues such as:

▲ Relocation: cultural, economic and business overview
▲ Economy and politics: information on political and economic structures to help conduct business successfully
▲ Immigration and tax.

Apart from improving your knowledge of international business, there is also the question of your personal self-development. We know that personality characteristics are relatively stable, but they can change over time, particularly after experiencing major life events. It is therefore useful to review your personality characteristics and behavior in terms of strengths and weaknesses to ask what makes you effective in particular environments and what areas you have to develop further.

Most organizations believe that prior international experience guarantees success in future international work. Consequently, they select international managers simply on the basis of their prior experience. However, empirical research has shown that international experience *per se* is not a good predictor for future success in international assignments (Torbiörn, 1982).

A manager may have had international experience, but this in itself does not mean that they have had a *successful* international experience. We all know people who seem highly 'global' (culturally sensitive, flexible, with a strong range of interests), but we also all know people who have worked abroad and are still parochial and narrow minded. They may know the food, but they don't know anything about the real life of the country and its people.

There is also the question of whether we can assume a universal international competence or whether some individuals are more suited to a specific culture or geographic location. For instance, a manager who has been successful in Mexico may not necessarily be successful in Thailand.

Nevertheless, most experts assume that there are some generic characteristics that can equip you for the international challenge. Personality characteristics and attitudes that are frequently mentioned in the context of international competence are empathy, openness, flexibility, self-confidence and self-possession, optimism, independence, initiative and intelligence (Gertsen, 1990). Attitudes that do not work well in international assignments are excessive use of stereotypes and prejudices or strong ethnocentrism (the tendency to see one's own culture and values as the only appropriate way of life).

What criteria do companies look for when they evaluate a manager's potential for taking on an international role? My survey of personnel managers in 83 internationally operating companies in Germany (Marx, 1996b) showed that they look for the characteristics outlined in Table 16.

Most of these attributes are 'soft' factors: social competence, adaptability, openness, flexibility and self-reliance. Consequently, selection that is mainly based on technical or managerial skills is not sufficient.

*Table 16 Desirable characteristics of international managers
(in order of priority)*

Social competence
Openness to other ways of thinking
Cultural adaptation
Professional excellence
Language skills
Flexibility
Ability to manage/work in a team
Self-reliance/independence
Mobility
Ability to deal with stress
Adaptability of the family
Patience
Sensitivity

These characteristics reinforce the assumptions of the culture shock triangle. It is necessary to work on the emotional side (ability to deal with stress), the thinking side (openness to other ways of thinking, flexibility, language skills) and the social side (social competence, ability to manage, cultural adaptation) in order to be effective in international business.

My coaching work with international managers also suggests that it is useful to think about the following characteristics before you start to evaluate your own ability to 'make it' internationally by using the questionnaire in Chapter 10: successful international executives seem to be able to reserve judgment, they are not absolute in their evaluation and they can apply flexibility. They know that some things cannot be objectified and are beyond rationality. They are more interested in analyzing a situation as an aid to further action than in spending time reflecting on why things are not like they are at home (Ratin, 1983). Many of these characteristics are related to the way people think, but they also have an emotional momentum: the ability to cope with uncertainty or ambiguity.

Some companies offer a development package to their international managers consisting of assessment and coaching for an international role. As a consultant, I have developed a service that is increasingly being used by global organizations. Assessments for international work are in-depth and take a minimum of half a day, with the following format:

▲ Psychological interviews that probe the motivation for going abroad, social skills and cultural sensitivity
▲ Personality questionnaires
▲ Psychoanalytically oriented techniques.

This process allows a comprehensive evaluation of candidates by using different methods. Assessments are followed up by a feedback session where all the results are discussed with the manager and recommendations for further development are made. Managers and companies receive a full report of the assessment and use the information for long-term development. A case study will illustrate this approach:

A company selected a high-flying employee from the UK for a senior assignment. The manager had never worked at international level and his company wanted an evaluation of his international potential.
The assessment brought out several concerns:

▲ *This manager took a very cautious approach and did not show any orientation towards taking a risk. How would he deal with the uncertainty of international work?*
▲ *He was shy and felt uncomfortable in most unfamiliar social situations. How would he establish contacts at work and outside?*
▲ *He was easily affected by his feelings and showed a tendency to worry. Was he sufficiently stress resistant?*

This was a situation where the prospective assignee needed more time to develop into the new role. His company had originally planned to send him abroad with a week's notice. This assignment did not in fact happen.

Very few assessments result in such serious concerns. More often, development issues are isolated which can be immediately targeted, thereby improving effectiveness. The next case shows such an example:

A highly experienced international manager was recommended to start up a new operation in South East Asia. The company wanted to give the manager as much support as possible and suggested an assessment and coaching session.

The assessment session showed the following results. As could be expected from his past experience, this manager exhibited strong cross-cultural sensitivity and the ability to deal with a great deal of pressure. However, the assessment also uncovered several issues for his future development:

▲ *As this was a start-up operation, it was recommended that the candidate should develop a stronger entrepreneurial orientation.*
▲ *The candidate was highly socially motivated and needed a lot of recognition by his organization. He would have to have an occasional 'pat on the back' and strong support lines.*
▲ *His job commitment was so high that one could question whether he had a sufficiently balanced lifestyle. He therefore had to reevaluate the way he lived.*
▲ *His conceptual understanding of international management could be improved and he could work on stronger perspective taking.*
▲ *He needed more training in negotiating skills.*

The company used these findings in the following way:

▲ *Immediately, to complement him with someone with a stronger entrepreneurial orientation.*
▲ *To set up clear support structures during the assignment.*
▲ *To explain the stress model of adaptation and explore non-work-related activities.*
▲ *To offer individual cross-cultural coaching and organize a reading list to improve his conceptual understanding of cross-cultural management.*

▲ *Longer term, to send him on a training course in negotiation.*

Management development sessions with an international angle may be useful for your own preparation. A typical approach is summarized below.

Part One: Half-day psychological assessment

Aim

Assessment of characteristics that are relevant for cross-cultural adaptation. These include sensitivity to different cultures, adaptability to new situations, communication, relationship skills, people orientation, stress resistance, self-reliance, result and action orientation.

Methods
▲ Structured interview
▲ Psychoanalytically oriented techniques
▲ Personality questionnaires targeting values and coping mechanisms.

Part Two: Coaching session
(another half-day as a minimum)

Feedback
▲ Analysis of assessment results
▲ Strengths and weaknesses in relation to cross-cultural adaptation
▲ Self-awareness and awareness of own cultural 'baggage'.

Coaching
▲ Exercise: international management situations
▲ Analysis of answers and description of cross-cultural model
▲ Analysis of differences in cultural values
▲ Personal/family situation and process of adaptation.

The best advice is to take a proactive and positive approach to your own career management and not to rely on your organization to provide everything for you.

Making a smooth return

Your professional reentry should be planned right from the start of a long-term international assignment, irrespective of whether you have a guaranteed job to go back to or not. Take the following steps:

▲ First of all, check whether a job is guaranteed on return and the range of jobs that may be offered by the organization. Get any guarantee in writing.

▲ Discuss with a career adviser/mentor/personnel department in your company how they see your reintegration on return. If you plan to come back to the same organization (which ideally you should and, ideally, your organization should be interested in), try to come back at least once a year and spend some time in headquarters and with the personnel department looking at future job options. This is also an important time to advertise your successes and to show your interest in a variety of possible jobs.

▲ Organize a mentor (not your line manager!) before an international assignment. Having a senior manager as your mentor is not only important for discussing management situations while you are abroad, but also in terms of long-term career planning.

▲ Discuss potential job openings with your company in the last year of your assignment – at the latest six months before your return. You have to be proactive and cannot expect job opportunities to be given to you automatically.

▲ Companies are changing at an incredible speed nowadays and often returning expatriates don't recognize the organization they once worked for. Therefore, stay in touch with headquarters via all possible routes.

My colleague Jerry Gray at Norman Broadbent International gives the following advice to job seekers on returning to their home country:

*"Handling applications remotely is very difficult. It is a real dis-
advantage to be far away and not being available for interviews.
Very few companies would fly candidates in, unless there is no one
else who can compete. As communications improve day by day,
such as videoconferencing etc., this may change. Nevertheless,
people may miss out because they are not available for early interviews. If you live abroad, you may not have full access to all
recruitment media and you have to rely on fewer publications.*

*Ideally, one should come back from abroad with time to spare
in order to find the next role, something that will fit well. Responsible companies should allow a three-month repatriation period
(maybe on reduced salary) with use of their facilities in order to
allow their managers to find new jobs if they cannot guarantee
jobs on return.*

*Returning managers should tap into contacts in recruitment
consultancies; approach the top 10 consultancies in your country
and in your field. Target recruitment consultants who have international experience themselves. These consultants are more aware
of the difficulties of coming back and may be more sympathetic in
giving you their time and advice.*

*The rest is very much as one would recommend to any job
seeker: approach companies that are of interest, study all job
advertisements and do a lot of networking. Networking should
include external as well as internal contacts. In large organizations, it takes a lot of internal networking to find the right job. "*

An international manager in banking who had been working in
various European countries supported this last point:

*"I believe repatriation is a major problem. I came back from
France to a good job but coming back from abroad the second
time, I was uncomfortable for the first two years after my return.
The human resource department in my company was looking to
find me a new job and I also did a lot of networking. In the end, I
managed to find my current position in the same company simply
through persistence and networking. Luckily, this new position fits
my professional background extremely well. "*

The following comments describe the process of readaptation:

> "*I found that the inverse culture shock was quite strong: London is more frantic and in London, the company expects you to impress. One has to be much more proactive in comparison to Japan where the boss tells you what to do and work is relatively reactive. In a way, it is real life here in London.*"

> "*Repatriation – there was a formal interview panel for my career progression but this was not properly followed up. When I pushed, they offered me a job in the investment arm of the bank. This sounded initially very promising and looked good on my CV. Nevertheless, I found it difficult to come back. The job was not what I expected, I had more independence in France, I felt I was too senior for the job and was generally disillusioned. The central personnel department did not support me on relocation and the people clearly saw me as an asset in the company but did not treat me as an asset. Within three months of coming back, I decided to leave and I was actually recruited by one of my former clients in France.*"

Not all returns are sources of stress, however. Many international managers are quite clear that they only want to have a three-year assignment and are psychologically planning their return. Managers who have lived in more difficult countries ('hardship' places or in more 'alien' cultures) often experience a prolonged honeymoon period on return. These professionals often enjoyed the challenge of a more difficult assignment but are also happy to return to a more familiar environment. Coming back to a place where you can speak your native language may be experienced as a joy after a difficult foreign assignment.

Individuals vary in their perceptions. Some managers make themselves very unhappy by having unrealistic expectations of a fantastic job on return. Developing a pragmatic view (and this includes getting the facts about changes in the organization and opportunities) seems a better way to ensure a good return.

Although some managers have had top responsibilities in their foreign assignments, including negotiations with the most senior businesspeople and government ministers, it is simply not realistic to expect the same status on return to your home country.

How can you best use your international experience, at a personal as well as professional level? Personally, it certainly means an expansion of your social circle, your hobbies, interests and activities. Professionally, it means looking at a wider range of jobs, making sure that your own company understands the activities in which you have been involved overseas and that you market your new skills. If you are looking for a new job, try to sell your new international skills as much as possible. The good news is that our own work within the recruitment market has shown that managers who have been on international assignments tend to earn higher salaries than those without international experience.

Tips for cross-border applicants

If you decide to apply for a job in a different country, it is advisable to adapt your application style to the style of the country to which you are applying. In a survey of 300 job applicants for management positions in France, Germany and the UK, I found enormous differences in style.

French applicants generally use handwritten cover letters. This may be in response to the widespread use of graphological analysis by French companies in the selection process. Other characteristics of the French include:

▲ Always listing personal interests
▲ Standard layout of CV
▲ Listing languages spoken
▲ Occasionally including a photo.

German applicants often include their parents' personal details and occupation. Against the stereotype, they seem least likely to follow a clear structure and format in their CV presentation. Other characteristics of the Germans are:

▲ Always attaching a photo
▲ Sometimes including references from previous employers

▲ Attaching copies of all academic and professional certificates
▲ Rarely listing personal interests
▲ Listing languages spoken.

British candidates rarely list foreign languages, probably reflecting the fact that in the UK speaking a second language fluently is unusual. Other characteristics of the British include:

▲ Writing the longest CVs (up to 10 pages)
▲ Rarely attaching a photo
▲ Occasionally listing other interests.

Planning a successful international career

▲ Be proactive in getting international experience, whether it is a short-term or a long-term assignment.
▲ Choose assignments carefully: assess the risk factors as well as the skills and competencies you will develop on the assignment, and the significance of the assignment for the company.
▲ Even if you don't have a concrete career goal, assess the long-term implications of the specific assignment for your future career.
▲ Assess what you need from the organization.
▲ Get external advice on the package you are being offered.
▲ Get tax advice.
▲ Carry out a self-assessment of your personality (see Chapter 10).
▲ Ask for training (management development and cross-cultural) and family support.
▲ Define and agree ongoing support (clear reporting lines and expectations on both sides).
▲ Plan your repatriation (ideally, get a job guaranteed or, if not, get the organization to offer career counseling and help with finding a suitable position).
▲ Find a mentor in the organization.
▲ Engage in self-development activities: read a lot of international management literature, read the international press, get as much local exposure as possible.

▲ Deal positively with the stress and emotional upheaval that some international work involves.
▲ Improve your language skills.
▲ Ultimately, develop curiosity and flexibility in your thinking.

8

Managing International Managers

Most companies are fully aware that an important factor in international expansion and competitiveness is the development of effective international managers. Yet many assignments are failures: managers don't adapt overseas, families have problems with their new lifestyle, there are difficulties in negotiations and in joint ventures. How do organizations see their responsibilities towards their international managers and their families? How can they select and develop the right kind of managers and ensure their successful career development and repatriation?

When I started working in this area, there was little information on representative human resource practices in international business. I decided to collect my own data and published a report on international human resource practices in the UK and Germany in 1996. The main findings of this report are summarized here, as they reflect a best-practice approach to international assignments.

Unfortunately, British and German companies currently do very little to help individuals and their families cope with international assignments. The survey looked at 92 internationally operating companies in each country. The majority of these companies sent employees to Europe and other continents. Very few companies (only 9.8 percent of the total) restricted their international assignments to Europe. The average assignment length was three years.

From a best-practice point of view, the aspects of international HR management detailed in Table 17 were of particular interest in the different stages of an international assignment, and these were targeted in the survey.

Table 17 Areas investigated in the survey

Selection
▲ What is the selection process?
▲ What are the criteria for selection and do companies have a list of competencies for international assignments?
▲ Do companies use psychological assessments to achieve an objective and comprehensive evaluation of adaptation skills?
▲ Do they involve the spouse at selection stage and address dual-career issues?

Preparation and training
▲ Do companies offer 'look-see' visits?
▲ Do they arrange language training?
▲ Do they provide cross-cultural training?

Ongoing support
▲ What type of support is provided by headquarters or on location?
▲ Do companies have a mentor system to facilitate international effectiveness and help with general career development?

Repatriation
▲ Do companies guarantee a job on return?

Based on information from the 184 companies involved in the survey, the results found are listed in Table 18 (Marx, 1996b).

Table 18 Main results of international HR survey in UK and Germany

	UK (%)	Germany (%)
Selection		
Systematic use of international competencies	20.1	15.6
Systematic use of psychological testing	15.2	4.4
Interview with spouse at selection stage	4.3	15.3
Preparation and training		
Offer of look-see visits	67.0	59.3
Offer of language training	85.0	91.0
Offer of cultural training	44.4	44.6
Ongoing support		
Provided by headquarters or on location	83.9	83.8
Mentor system	21.3	28.9
Repatriation		
Guaranteed job on return	35.6	88.8

From these figures, we can see gaps at every stage of an international assignment process. The majority of companies seem to treat international work as if their managers were working in their home country.

Selection

Most companies still base their selection decisions purely on technical abilities and do not consider the individual's ability to adapt to working abroad. Only a minority of companies have a clear set of criteria against which they evaluate the potential of their managers to be successful in international work. 'Soft' issues, such as cultural sensitivity, flexibility, adaptability and so on, are rarely evaluated at this stage and few companies use psychological assessments in relation to these international characteristics.

Similarly, although the number of dual-career couples is on the increase and organizations noted this explicitly in my research, the influence of spouse and family is largely ignored at the selection stage.

However, there are moves towards more progressive practices in British and German companies. The following comments show some of the more effective approaches to selection:

> *"Use of recently established list of competencies and development of psychological procedures to assess these competencies."*

> *"Adaptability – assessing how a person will fit into the different cultures."*

> *"We realized in the last year the need to get the spouse involved in the selection process, and intend to do so in the future."*

Preparation and training

Look-see visits and language training are offered by most companies – but not all. As one HR manager of an oil company reported:

> *"We don't offer look-see visits. If the manager knew where he was going, he would never take the job."*

Cross-cultural training was offered by fewer than half of the interviewed companies. Managers often receive advice on tax, benefits or housing, but are not offered cross-cultural training. Some companies believe that it is sufficient to provide a country report as the sole means of preparation. On the positive side, there is a trend in many companies towards reviewing their training and preparation and identifying effective modules of cross-cultural training.

According to Brewster (1991), US companies use pre-departure training programs less frequently than do European and Japanese firms. This lack of cross-cultural training may contribute to the high expatriate failure rate of US managers, estimated at between 25 and 40 percent.

A research report on behalf of the European Commission, *European Expatriates in China*, makes several recommendations for better preparation. It suggests sending expatriates on short courses in China about six months after the posting starts to help overcome culture shock (Campbell, 1996).

Ongoing support

A mentor system is rarely used to help managers with their future career development. Although most companies commented that they provide ongoing support either through headquarters or on location, the type of support varies significantly: for some companies it is merely 'the manager has our fax and telephone number', whereas others favor close communication and will have a weekly exchange. Similarly, some companies are very clear in establishing the reporting lines and the number of expected contacts with headquarters, while others are fairly vague about their expectations.

Repatriation

There is an interesting cross-cultural difference in relation to repatriation. Whereas most UK companies are now not able to guarantee a position on return, the majority of German companies still do. However, German companies probably have to guarantee jobs on return in order to attract employees for foreign assignments in the first place (compare the discussion in Chapter 3 on Germans' dislike of ambiguity and need for security).

Main problems in international assignments

The three most frequently reported problems in the UK were:

Failure/performance problems/adaptation problems
▲ "People not comfortable with integrating in different cultures."
▲ "Some expatriates couldn't settle overseas."
▲ "Coming to grips with the culture."

Spouse
▲ "Relocating to the USA where the spouse cannot work."
▲ "Spouse not settling in."

Repatriation
▲ "Managing the expectations of returning secondees."
▲ "Finding the right jobs on returning."

In contrast, German companies reported the following major problems:

Repatriation
▲ "Loss of status."
▲ "Readaptation to the hierarchical system in Germany."
▲ "The family has to be 'resocialized' in relation to high expectations of standard of living and loss of salary."

Spouse/family
▲ "Professional activity of partner becomes a problem."
▲ "Important to develop programs for partners."
▲ "Family may not be adaptable."

Compensation and benefits
▲ "Problems with tax and social security."

What the best companies do

Before discussing the negative findings, let us look at two case examples from Germany and the UK. These survey responses show what the more progressive companies do in managing their international managers.

The German company gave the responses in Table 19 and the UK company those in Table 20.

Table 19 Survey responses from German company

Number of employees abroad	Over 300
In what countries	Worldwide
When did you start to send employees abroad	Since beginning of the 1950s
What is the duration of an international assignment	5 years, slightly shorter for younger people

Selection methods

Do you have a list of competencies for international work	Yes
Do you use psychological tests	Yes, use of assessment center for international managers
Is the family involved	No

Training

Do you organize look-see visits	Yes
Do you organize language training	Yes
Do you organize intercultural training	Yes

Support

Do you have a mentor system	No

Repatriation

Do you guarantee a job	Offer of career counseling
What are the main problems	Repatriation: the longer the international manager has been abroad, the more difficult the reintegration
What are new developments in international HR	More transnational exchange (i.e. full two-way exchange), more short-term international work as opposed to expatriation, more flexible and less formalized procedures
What do you think are the characteristics of international managers	Good listening ability, preparedness to learn, negotiation skills, helicopter view

Table 20 Survey responses from UK company

Number of employees abroad	Several thousand
In what countries	Worldwide
What is the duration of an international assignment	4 years, after which 60 percent go back to their own countries and as many as 40 percent go to other countries

Selection methods

Do you have a list of competencies for international work	Not yet, but is presently being prepared
Do you use psychological tests	No

Training

Do you organize look-see visits	On rare occasions
Do you organize language training	Yes, but often this is not taken up as in most countries you can get by without language
Do you organize intercultural training	If possible

Support

Type of ongoing support	Support from local departments
Do you have a mentor system	No

Repatriation

Do you guarantee a job	No, but the minimum is a redundancy payment
What are the main problems	Spouse's career
What are new developments in international HR	Greater assistance to the spouse to find employment and stronger educational advice

What managers think

When I interviewed a group of international managers about how they perceived their selection and training, the following trends were evident:

Selection
▲ In the majority of cases, organizations use relatively rough-and-ready selection methods. For example, 19 percent of the managers were not even interviewed but simply asked to go abroad.
▲ One manager said that her selection was an act of desperation. She was selected because her organization had been trying for two years to fill the job.
▲ In no cases were the family or partner included in the selection process:

> *"It was mostly self-selection. Overseas assignments are seen as rewards by most companies. If you played the right company politics, you got the job. This is particularly important when it comes to repatriation. The family situation was never considered in any of the selections I went through."*

▲ In many cases, international managers were proactive and established contact with the foreign subsidiary beforehand.
▲ Very few companies looked beyond technical ability and included psychological assessment to establish international adaptability.

Training
▲ 82 percent of the managers did not receive any preparation in terms of country briefing or cross-cultural training. Language training was rarely given.
▲ Some managers were proactive in terms of carrying out their own research on the country.

Managers' comments on training included the following:

> *"I had no training at all. The idea was just to get on the plane and go."*

> *"Our company has a very multinational workforce and therefore does not assume that particular training is necessary."*

> *"None. I had to find my own place to live."*

> *"From the UK end, they sent me to cross-cultural training which was useful for my wife but not for myself since I knew the French culture well. On the French side, there was no help even in finding the house. In France, they had not had an expatriate before and there was a big cost argument about the case. The French felt they were imposed upon. This situation was entirely different from Singapore, where there were many more expatriates."*

> *"I had an extended three-month preparation phase. This training consisted of country briefing, learning a new method for the planning of projects, communication skills, particularly in the cross-cultural area, language training, consulting techniques and a short computer training."*

> *"I was given a two-and-a-half day country briefing/cross-cultural training organized by an American company. This was a company that was founded by expatriates. They offer an orientation to understand cultural values and different perspectives. What I found particularly useful was a panel discussion with couples who had been abroad and covering such issues as having children overseas and the aspects of moving. Before this orientation, my wife did not seem so confident about the move. The briefing provided something like a stronger comfort level for both of us."*

This predominantly depressing picture is unfortunately repeated when considering the type of support managers received during the assignment. Approximately half of the international managers surveyed did not have sufficient support either from headquarters or from the foreign subsidiary. These findings suggest that managers have to take a proactive approach in order to ensure that they receive sufficient training and support in their international work.

However, don't automatically adopt a negative view of your own company. I have met many international managers who had (objectively) good support but were still negative about the support they received. Often managers expect too much from their organizations and are not sufficiently proactive. My advice is to ask for what you want!

Companies want you to succeed in your international work and they will therefore give you reasonable support and preparation if they believe that this will help you, and if you have a convincing negotiation style. Even companies that have relatively fixed expatriate policies seem flexible enough to accommodate individual requirements.

Meeting managers' expectations

One study of 85 expatriates of 12 nationalities working in 25 different countries is a good illustration of the need for organizations to understand and meet their managers' expectations (Van Ruitenbeek, Manchester School of Management, UMIST, 1998). The study investigated the factors that would affect expatriates' motivation to perform and stay with the company. The findings show that work adjustment, living adjustment and family adjustment are closely related. Moreover, job satisfaction is positively related to perceived organizational support and satisfaction with local living conditions. A neglect of the 'softer' factors – including support in terms of living conditions and family – may negatively affect the degree of work adjustment and therefore performance.

What do managers expect and value in their expatriate package? Expatriates in Van Ruitenbeek's study claimed that the factors listed in Table 21 were most important in relation to their finances, job support and family support.

Table 21 Important factors in the expatriate package

Financial aspects	Job support	Family support
Medical insurance	Clear objectives	Orientation visit
Removal costs	Face-to-face briefing	(pre-departure)
Relocation allowance	Written information	Cross-cultural training
Housing allowance	Cross-cultural training	Orientation to local
Travel and subsistence		community
allowance		Home leave
		Help with repatriation

A manager would be off to a productive start in an international assignment if these conditions were agreed to and met.

Recommendations for best practice

Defining international competencies

As with any managerial competencies, companies have to decide how much time and effort they want to spend on defining international competencies. Whereas it is essential for competencies to be related to the business strategy (that is, specifying the type of manager the organization needs to implement the strategy), I would not recommend spending too much time on their definition. Many organizations expend a vast amount of resources on refining their competency framework, only to find that the competencies are already outdated by the time they have been finalized. A more economical approach is to look at generic competencies that are important in international management and to add specific ones that may reflect your particular business strategy.

In my own assessments of international managers, I often use the criteria in Table 22, defined on the basis of the existing management literature and my practical experience.

Table 22 International competencies

Sensitivity to different cultures
▲ Open approach to other cultures
▲ Cultural awareness and sensitivity
▲ Interest in international business

Adaptability to new situations
▲ Ability to cope with unstructured and ambiguous situations
▲ Flexibility in thinking
▲ Communication and relationship skills
▲ Language skills and aptitude for learning new languages

People orientation
▲ Empathic behavior
▲ Interpersonal sensitivity and listening skills
▲ Assertiveness
▲ Ability to work in international teams
▲ Negotiation skills
▲ Leadership style

Stress resistance
▲ Self-confidence
▲ Effective coping style

Self-reliance
▲ Ability to make decisions and to operate independently

What do organizations look for in their future leaders? From my research in the top 200 UK companies, it seems that most organizations still focus on the classic senior management competencies (such as management style, flexibility, responsibility and business skills), but do not include international competencies, despite their global operations (Marx and Demby, 1998). More progressive companies use competencies such as multicultural awareness, risk management, networking, customer focus and management of information systems.

Attracting the right candidate

As for all new jobs, organizations need to offer a realistic outline of the position. Recruitment advertisements should therefore be carefully phrased in order to attract the right type of candidate and set the correct expectations. This could be a particular problem when seeking candidates for so-called hardship or more difficult places. Putting too many palm trees into a job advertisement for the Middle East, for example, does not project a realistic image of the job or the location – it is not a holiday destination but a place that can be seen as restrictive by western standards. Michael Pert, HR Manager of Savola (Saudi Arabia), commented:

"The Middle East is not the most attractive place to go to as far as international assignments are concerned. Culture and religion are inextricably linked and therefore one has to address the fear and apprehension that western candidates may experience. Most recruiters use highly attractive advertisements but they also have to be realistic. One has to point out the positives as people don't just wake up one morning and think: 'I want to go to Saudi Arabia'. However, one also has to be careful not to attract the salary hunters but to get people who want to have an international career, who are keen to learn something new and are not purely salary driven."

Savola succeeds in attracting international talent by advertising its fast growth and progressive management cultures, a real fusion of the latest western management techniques and Islamic/Middle Eastern values.

Although the traditional hardship places with their lack of infrastructure and social isolation may be disappearing, we seem to be confronted with a new type of hardship place that requires a special, frontier type of manager: low-security countries with a high risk of abduction and kidnapping. The abduction of international executives is on the increase; it is estimated that the number of kidnappings worldwide has doubled in the last few years.

The worst zones are Latin America, Russia and the Commonwealth of Independent States. International organizations nowadays often take out insurance policies against kidnapping.

Assessing international adaptability

Most companies look for a 'magic' assessment tool (ideally a 10-minute questionnaire) to evaluate international adaptability, but this will not provide a reliable and valid assessment. Because of the complexity of international work, it is unlikely that one questionnaire, particularly a short one, will give you answers to the complex question of how a manager will adapt and perform at an international level. To answer this question, more in-depth procedures are needed.

Assessment centers at graduate entry

More and more organizations now include situational exercises with a cross-cultural content in their assessment centers if they want to select graduates for an international career. Typically, these assessment centers are developed by external consultants with experience in this area.

Internationally oriented assessment centers are also used at a more senior level in the context of development centers. These try to identify the development needs of managers, attention to which will ultimately help them progress to senior management. The results are used for personal and career development. As part of the international expansion of many organizations, an international component, similar to assessment centers for graduates, is often included.

Structured interviews and self-selection

As a first step, it makes sense to conduct structured interviews to identify managers who are mobile and have a positive attitude towards an international assignment. There are ways to help managers to self-select and to decide themselves whether they really want to work internationally, whether on long-term or short-term assignments. For example, Employment Conditions Abroad (ECA) has developed a computerized system to help managers consider all the aspects of taking on an international assignment.

Psychological assessment of international potential

An in-depth psychological assessment of international potential does not rely on a single questionnaire but consists of different methods. Many organizations only have one person who is technically capable of a particular assignment and therefore feel that no selection issues are involved. However, in such situations I would still suggest that a risk assessment be carried out. Organizations need to know how likely it is that person will succeed, what their risk areas are, what development needs the manager should target and what type of support the organization should ideally provide. Different countries show different attitudes to using psychological assessment, particularly at a senior level. Whereas psychological assessment is frequently used at senior level in the UK, for example, it is less frequent in the USA, France and Germany. However, even in these latter countries, interest in these methods is increasing, probably as a consequence of the internationalization of HR.

Psychological assessments are not interpreted in isolation from other job factors. The results of a psychological assessment have to be interpreted in the context of the type of job and the culture, the organizational support provided and the family factors. An interview with the spouse is often carried out to complement the manager's assessment.

Psychological assessment of foreign nationals

The internationalization of business increases the number of occasions when candidates of different nationalities are being considered for the same job.

Imagine you are an American manager interviewing a French candidate for your company in Boston. The French candidate speaks excellent English and soon you are discussing and testing his technical skills. Despite a great deal of common ground, you find it difficult to gauge the candidate: his choice of words is non-American, his presentation style and non-verbal behavior do not make instant sense and, at the end, you still have no idea of what type of person he is and whether he would fit into your company.

It is hard to evaluate foreign nationals in a job interview because our usual, cultural-specific anchors and terms of reference do not apply. In this situation, psychological assessment can be extremely useful in complementing the traditional interview process, because it provides objective terms of reference.

International companies often assume that foreign nationals who speak good English should be able to undergo the normal assessment process in that language. This is a serious mistake. It not only disadvantages non-native English speakers in terms of ability tests, but also in terms of the personality characteristics that you are trying to assess.

Ideally, you should administer tests in the candidate's native language. Apart from specific testing techniques, you have to consider how familiar candidates are with assessment procedures in general. In some cultures, assessments for selection or development are simply not acceptable and therefore their use will not make sense to the managers involved. Multinationals find it difficult to introduce assessment concepts in cultures such as the Middle East, where individual competitiveness is discouraged by the collectivism of the culture. In other cultures, managers will not understand why they have to comply with the time limit of the ability tests.

Also, psychological constructs and characteristics are not the same in all cultures, that is, they are not universally valid. For example, emotional states are expressed in different ways. Depression is related to negative affects and thinking in western cultures, whereas in traditional Chinese society it is more likely to be expressed in terms of physical symptoms; this may change as China becomes more westernized.

A few rules of thumb may lead to a fairer assessment of foreign nationals:

▲ Find out whether assessment is used in the culture concerned. If not, give candidates a thorough introduction to the process before the assessment day.
▲ Carry out the assessment in the candidate's native language. If this is not feasible because there are no existing tests, use tests in English if the candidate is sufficiently fluent (but apply statistical corrections for the fact that English is not the mother tongue).
▲ Compare the candidate's scores with the norms for the relevant country.

Dual-career issues and children's education

Although the existence of a spouse with a career crucially affects a manager's future mobility, very few organizations address this issue at the moment. As a minimum, I would recommend conducting an interview with the spouse before the assignment. Managers and their spouses often give different accounts of the family situation. Interviews with the spouse will show how positive they are about the forthcoming assignment, how supportive they are and, if there are two careers involved, what can be done to help the spouse. As described before, how well the spouse adapts is a significant factor in the success of an international assignment.

As outlined in Chapter 6, Shell International has a progressive support program in place. This combines financial support if the spouse wants to take further training with a comprehensive advisory service for families (medical advice, housing, schooling, etc.).

Some organizations think that one way of dealing with the dual-career issue is to reimburse the couple for the loss of the partner's income if they cannot work abroad. Often, however, it is not to do with finance, but rather a personal or lifestyle problem if the spouse cannot work. In such situations, it makes more sense to help the spouse find a suitable position abroad or offer them some external career counseling regarding what they are able to do and how this could fit in with their overall career.

Similarly, school facilities for children should be checked with relocation companies to facilitate the family's international mobility. Although most American expatriates may want to send their children to US or international schools, for example, there is also a trend towards sending children to local schools to give them maximum exposure to the new culture and improve their language skills.

Effective cross-cultural preparation

Companies currently prepare international managers in three ways (see Table 23). Ideally, all three should be combined, particularly for significant positions such as senior roles in joint ventures or setting up operations in a new country.

Table 23 Types of cross-cultural preparation

Minimum preparation	Country briefing
Intermediate preparation	Standard cross-cultural training (as in group training programs)
In-depth preparation	Individual coaching

Country briefings give an overview of conditions and can either be delivered through short group programs or simply by doing background reading.

Country briefing documents cover essential, up-to-date information and give a fast orientation. For example, the ECA's *Lifestyle Guide to Libya* covers the following sections:

▲ The territory
▲ The people
▲ The state
▲ The economy
▲ Money
▲ Services
▲ Time and leisure
▲ Housing
▲ Education
▲ Health and hygiene
▲ Clothing
▲ Shopping
▲ Food and drink
▲ Travel and hotels
▲ Immigration procedures and customs formalities
▲ Home-country rights and duties
▲ Addresses and information sources.

Country briefing reports are available from different organizations, of which ECA is one. There are also various books on living and working in particular countries. Some organizations, such as Cable &

Wireless, have developed their own briefing documents for the 43 countries in which they operate. Another type of international briefing that is consistently underused is companies' own informal network of returning employees.

Standard cross-cultural training is often given in the form of group programs, dealing with the history and social background of the country, particular customs, the business culture, social behavior, style of business negotiations, etc. These can be very effective programs, lasting anything from one day to several days.

Cross-cultural training programs are offered by a variety of organizations. In the UK, the Centre for International Briefing at Farnham Castle is one of the main organizers. Courses offered include:

▲ Four-day pre-departure courses for Africa, Asia, the Middle East, Latin America, the Caribbean and the Pacific islands.
▲ Two-day pre-departure courses for North America, eastern and western Europe.
▲ Two-day post-arrival courses for the UK.
▲ Special briefings on demand, normally two to three days, designed to meet the particular needs of organizations or individuals at short notice.

Courses include lectures and discussions on politics, economics, culture, language, doing business internationally, social constraints, customs and leisure. Spouses/partners are encouraged to participate.

A four-day course on South East Asia and the Far East includes the following components:

▲ Country focus/people and society
▲ Introduction to the language
▲ 'The other half' – situation of the spouse/partner
▲ Doing business in country X
▲ Finance for the UK expatriate
▲ Working and living in country X
▲ Cross-cultural communication skills
▲ Family life
▲ Health and hygiene in a warm climate

▲ Religion
▲ Adapting to a new environment.

In Germany, the Interkulturelles Training Center in Bad Honnef offers preparation programs, and in the Netherlands the Center for International Business Studies (CIBS), headed by Fons Trompenaars and based in Amstelveen, offers specific training in business-related topics. Programs include business briefings, seminars, workshops and specialized business topics such as:

▲ Cultural awareness
▲ Negotiating skills across cultures
▲ Managing across cultures
▲ Intercultural communication and teamwork
▲ Organizational culture and effectiveness
▲ Cultural aspects of mergers and acquisitions.

Courses are individually tailored to specific organizations.
    The aims of all of these standard group programs are the following:

▲ To learn about the politics, economics and working environment of the destination country
▲ To understand local business practices/attitudes and the culture of the host country
▲ To learn how local colleagues will perceive the international manager and their expectations
▲ To develop an understanding of how to cope in a new environment
▲ To learn about living conditions (including schools, health and leisure facilities).

What group programs cannot easily target is a better understanding of yourself (of your own characteristics, preferences, attitudes, values, etc.). But a strong knowledge of yourself and your attitudes is surely a prerequisite for understanding other people and different cultures.
    This is addressed in individual coaching. These sessions focus on the cross-cultural manager's personality and style and the particular

position. This preparation is primarily used for senior executives. It can also be helpful in preparing for negotiations as well as for working internationally from a home base (as the example of such a program in Chapter 7 showed).

A new form of intercultural training has been created in Germany that uses a CD-ROM, called the Delta Concept. Developed at the University of Duisburg in conjunction with other organizations, this interactive approach offers training in three areas in international business and management:

▲ Intercultural business communication
▲ Business negotiation
▲ Language skills for negotiating in English.

The Delta Concept is a self-study program and centers on a simulated negotiation between businesspeople from Germany, the UK and Spain. It is flexible and combines language training with training in business negotiation. The CD-ROM can be adapted to the user's own learning program and the most important issues for them. Alternatively, it is possible to learn more about negotiation and language skills and test your understanding of different cultural norms. For busy international managers who would like to improve their language skills as well as understanding these European business cultures, this is an interesting training method.

Getting the package right

Salaries and packages can be contentious issues. Compensation, tax and benefits for international assignments are becoming increasingly complex and organizations typically use external consultancy advice to get these right. There may also be pressure from managers to obtain the best package and benefits.

External consultancies such as ORC in the USA or Employment Conditions Abroad in the UK offer specialist services to help with salary issues. The international accountancy firms, such as Arthur Andersen, KPMG and Ernst & Young, have specialist services that advise on tax and international assignments. However, there are still many inconsistencies in international assignment packages and there is a particular need for more constructive tax advice.

At the same time, organizations have to be aware of 'salary hunters' in eastern Europe and the Middle East. Outsiders often suspect a certain arbitrariness in salary negotiations for international assignments and companies have to be careful not to apply an extremely individualist approach to salaries and benefits.

International career development

In the past, organizations have tried to attract and retain international managers by offering substantial packages. However, most organizations now try to equalize salaries between international and local managers and abolish expatriate status wherever possible. This is the right direction in terms of developing effective international teams, but it can make it difficult to attract, motivate and retain the right people.

As my work has shown, many of the UK's top 200 companies have recognized that executives are motivated by factors beyond remuneration. Personnel managers in large organizations know that their senior executives are looking for stimulating and challenging work and so understand that personal and career development are highly rated, as are international assignments. Senior managers seem to rate opportunities that the company can offer (such as personal development, international experience and job challenge) more highly than job security and remuneration. Organizations will need to develop more creative ways to motivate and retain their best managers (Marx and Demby, 1998).

In a typical three-year assignment, managers spend the first year finding their feet, in the second year they will perform at full speed, and in the third year they start to wind down as they are concerned with repatriation. In order to improve efficiency in the third year, it is in the organization's interest to help the manager concentrate on the job, either by guaranteeing a post on return or by offering a buffer period of a couple of months with full/reduced pay. Ideally, the organization should discuss career options once a year. One year before repatriation, a thorough career-counseling session should be undertaken. If the organization is not able to guarantee a job on return, it should arrange career counseling or an outplacement service for the returnee.

Large international companies sometimes have their own career-development unit. Cable & Wireless has a careers center in London that has background information on employers within the UK, useful organizations, networking activities, etc. Apart from being a library on career-related issues, the center employs external career consultants to help the company's managers.

There needs to be a balance between organizational support and encouraging managers to be proactive and take risks. Some organizations address this explicitly, as one senior executive illustrated when he compared international work to white water rafting! He only wanted to employ managers who were prepared to join a project that was not well structured and could have a variety of outcomes. This organization wanted to attract more entrepreneurial people who were able to take risks, not those who needed to feel secure at all times.

Some organizations believe that international managers are overly pampered, compared to some decades ago when "expatriates were sent out with no support and sometimes even had to build their own accommodation, they had to live in tents until they were able to build accommodation", as one manager in the oil industry commented.

Improving retention rates after international assignments

Many international managers leave the company after finishing an assignment. Sometimes this is because the company is not able to offer an appropriate job, but at other times it is because the returnee has been 'parked' in an inappropriate assignment or on extended project work. Many companies do not realize that successful international assignments represent a two-step climb in a manager's career. It is difficult and challenging to be effective in your own country, even more so in an alien culture.

The company has to match the expectations of the returning employee with available job opportunities. Companies are becoming concerned that they may lose their best international managers to their competitors if they do not manage returnees effectively.

Karen-Eve Pfotzer of Cable & Wireless listed the following retention tools, both during and after an assignment:

▲ Generous expatriate package
▲ Bonus plans and share options
▲ Employment 'insurance policy'
▲ Global tax and financial coaching support
▲ Excellent medical care and support
▲ Strong expatriate network
▲ Educational assistance for children
▲ Rest and relaxation travel funds
▲ Strong communication links via internal newsletters and international job adverts
▲ Management development courses
▲ Cultural briefings
▲ Family support
▲ Strong succession planning for the top 300 managers
▲ Career counseling and management
▲ Special courses at Cable & Wireless College
▲ HR support from six months before the assignment ends
▲ Redeployment 'grace period' of 12 weeks
▲ HR contact throughout redeployment
▲ Availability of external counsellors.

How does your organization match up to these recommendations?

9

Global Leadership

We all want to know how successful international executives broke through the culture shock and managed their careers. To this aim, I interviewed role models for every international manager: Peter Job (Chief Executive of Reuters), Sir Win Bischoff (Chairman of Citigroup Europe) and Edward Dolman (Group Chief Executive of Christie's). I chose these particular executives because they are leading top companies with international operations and because they all had successful international careers before becoming chief executive or chairman. This chapter describes their views and advice on global management, often in their own words. The interview with Edward Dolman focuses on the globalization of companies.

Peter Job, Chief Executive, Reuters

Educated at Exeter College, Oxford, BA in German and French. Joined Reuters in 1963 to take up a position as a journalist and was based in Paris, New Delhi, Kuala Lumpur, Jakarta and Buenos Aires from 1963 to 1978. Managed Reuters in Asia, based in Hong Kong between 1978 and 1990. Became a full main board director of Reuters in 1989. Since 1991 has been Chief Executive of Reuters Holdings plc.

What makes a good international manager?

"*Everybody starts off thinking their own national culture is best and, therefore, as an international manager you can never rest until you have discovered the positive characteristics of the new culture. Optimism is one of the major characteristics of a good international manager and this also includes optimism about the capabilities of others. It is extremely dangerous to underestimate the capability of others, but this is unfortunately what often happens in international business. I therefore see optimism as one of the major criteria of effective managers.*

Other prime characteristics are curiosity and a celebration of 'vive les differences!'. You need enthusiasm and interest in looking at the way things are done in an unfamiliar environment.

There is a propensity for cultures to think badly of one another. This was certainly the case when westerners tried to understand Japanese business. Because of differences in manners and business attitudes, westerners thought negatively of Japanese managers and obviously did not understand them or made an attempt to understand them. If you threw away these bags of stereotypes and prejudices, the foreign counterpart would be interested and would show and explain their side of doing business and their culture to you. For example, there was a common attitude among westerners to not even attempt to learn the Japanese language because of potential mistakes one could make, thereby offending one's negotiation partners. This is a complete stereotype and does not correspond to reality. It is always advantageous to speak the foreign language – not necessarily to conduct the whole business negotiation in that language but to show an interest and respect to others."

Timing

"*Another issue in international business is to know when the apple is ready to fall from the tree. This century has seen many changes. The last world war had a strong impact on nationalities seeing each other in a negative light. However, in international* business, it is not only the understanding of the other culture but also the timing that is of essence. It is clear that one has to choose one's target with care. Sometimes, the market of a particular country is simply not ready and, if it is ready, one has to move very quickly. The timing can also depend on the history of the country, for example whether the country is ready to embark on joint ventures with other countries.

This leads to three success criteria in international executives:

▲ Optimism
▲ Curiosity
▲ Sense of 'rightness' as far as the history of the country is concerned. "

Complexity of different markets

"We also have to realize that a complex culture is difficult to understand. It is difficult to build business in Germany and Japan. In both countries, you have very strong domestic businesses and it is therefore hard for outsiders to come in. Doing business in Germany and Japan is a good test of your ability to do business in a foreign market. Both Germany and Japan thrive on long-term business relationships and quality issues. If you succeed in those markets, this speaks for your long-term orientation and the quality issue of our own company. However, the biggest test is the US. The US does not instill a long-term business relationship. Anybody can go in there, especially if they have a new idea, but the pressure is intolerable. It is difficult to establish a business despite the open market and it is difficult to make a good acquisition because everybody is only selling on top of the market. To sum up, there are many difficulties in international business, but we also have to make the assumption that these can be overcome by taking a long-term view. "

Advice to international managers

"My advice focuses on the following three areas:

▲ *The manager needs a strong sense of his/her company and where the company is going, what the company stands for, etc.*

▲ *Ideally, the manager should aim to disappear into the background like a chameleon – adapting is making do with the material and the people he/she finds.*

▲ *You need strong leadership characteristics and independence as well as the ability to communicate enthusiasm about the job at hand. What is the difference to national leaders? The international leader needs on top of these characteristics a deeper knowledge of the company product. There is also a need for a connection between the center and the periphery; basically, you need someone with a very strong sense of activities in the center who can relay these to the periphery and the other way round. Therefore, as an international manager, you should never be too long on either side but balance your activities and positions between the periphery (foreign operation) and the center. "*

The latter point very much corresponds to Job's own career where he had fluctuated between going on three-year assignments and coming back to headquarters.

The difference between traditional managers and the 'new' international manager

"There is more stress on language now. Knowing the local language, even at its most basic, shows that there is some interest and commitment on the part of the manager. The international manager is no longer seen as 'God's gift to the world'. There is also a demystification in terms of understanding other cultures. Today, there is less interest in manners and more in attitudes. Whereas it is important to comply with some basic manners in cross-cultural meetings, more important is the attitude that conveys what one

wants and to come to the point. It is more important to have a positive attitude, trust and commitment to the business partner than to observe the rules of when to use tu *or* vous *in France.* **"**

Career planning

Job did not have a career plan. After his studies in French and German at Oxford University, he chose journalism because he wanted to travel. He worked as a journalist for seven years and progressed into administration by chance. In his own words, he never had a clear career plan but followed the opportunities that came up. In his case, the editor needed an assistant and this is how he got into administration and management.

His own career, with stints as a journalist in Paris, New Delhi, Kuala Lumpur, Jakarta, Buenos Aires, Hong Kong as well as being regional manager in Asia Pacific, suggests that he is universally adaptable. Job commented that he "never found anything repellent" and he obviously sustained a high level of interest and enthusiasm for foreign cultures. He added that he was lucky to focus on Asia and South America, which were both thriving economies and therefore interesting to do business in:

"*The problem is that if you don't like a group of people, you are not going to be successful.* **"**

His most successful assignment was probably setting up in the Asia Pacific region, including Japan. At the time, he was based in Hong Kong and the company had good products that he was able to exploit. He also had an excellent team with a strong mix of country management and specialist knowledge. As he commented:

"*If resources are scarce and there is a grand-scale operation, people have to pull together and there is not a lot of internal nagging going on.* **"**

Frequent international trips

As Chief Executive of Reuters, Job undertakes about 19 trips a year, which means about every two weeks he takes a trip abroad, all over the world. The intellectual demands of switching to different cultures in a short amount of time are not a great problem for him because he has been to most places. Physically, he has also adapted quite well in dealing with the pressures of frequent international traveling. He thinks that air travel is much better these days, he takes a good airline, travels first class and simply sleeps. His trick is to work normal hours at the other end and he therefore gets used to the change in time zones very fast.

> *"Reading about the history of the more important countries is a very good preparation. For example, if I wanted to know something on the topic of xenophobia in Russia, I would read how Russians have dealt with foreigners economically over several decades. Similarly, if I wanted to assess whether to make an investment in India, I have to understand something about the history and the politics in the last hundred years – the background to an overly bureaucratic system.*
>
> *If you are heading a regional operation, you have to understand the dynamics in the region and how neighbors see each other. For example, to understand the situation in North Asia, one has to know something about Russia, Korea, China and Japan. The relationship with immediate neighbors is important to know, similar to how asking company A about its competitors gives some understanding of that company."*

Comfort zones and comfort activities

> *"In international work, one needs to withdraw and have some privacy: it is like eating a foreign breakfast. People are most vulnerable at breakfast time and eating foreign breakfasts can be quite difficult. My worst breakfast was in Tibet, consisting of raw barley with buttermilk and sour tea. Nowadays I quite like eating a foreign breakfast and particularly enjoy the Japanese breakfast.*

> *It is difficult to be immersed 24 hours a day in a foreign cul-*
> *ture and you need some refuge. In my case, it was getting out to*
> *sea when I was in Hong Kong. This counterbalanced the over-*
> *crowding and tremendous buzz of Hong Kong.* **"**

His family enjoyed the opportunities that the many international assignments brought. Looking back, his wife thinks that it is wonderful to have had such a varied life. The children enjoyed traveling but, now that they are back in Britain, are concentrating on discovering their own culture.

Management literature

Job's first love is poetry rather than management literature:

> **"***This is partly due to the fact that American management liter-*
> *ature is so dominating and does not have much to say in terms of*
> *international business. However, my chairman sends me trend-*
> *setting articles which are important reading.* **"**

International managers in the year 2020

> **"***Travel will be less common and there will be much more use*
> *of videoconferencing. This will weaken the personal links with*
> *business partners and also the sense of what the customer mood*
> *is. If I want to know the customer's mood, I have a meeting with*
> *the customer. However, this will probably happen less*
> *frequently.*
>
> *People will become less mobile: spouses will simply not give*
> *up their jobs, particularly if they have important jobs. If this is the*
> *case, then truly international companies will have to seek some*
> *people who want an international career and want to move*
> *around. They will have to offer them great promotional aspects*
> *and they particularly have to recruit where the customer base is.*
> *For example, if a firm in New York has a major customer base in*
> *Europe, it needs to recruit more Europeans.*

Don't believe any advice to stay in your own country and 'cultivate your own garden', to use Voltaire's expression; growth will come from another place and you will have to pursue your whole career with that attitude. "

Commentary

▲ Job gives strong warnings against underestimating others' ability and the propensity to think negatively about other nations. There are probably two reasons for this: first, it is the 'in group' versus the 'out group' differentiation that makes us think negatively about people who do not belong to our group. Secondly, there is a personal element in downgrading others. Psychologists have shown that people with low self-esteem often try to enhance their esteem by looking down on others and by carrying out 'downward' comparisons. This attitude not only puts you on a bad footing with potential business partners because of the lack of respect, but it also makes it impossible for you to learn more about the other culture and your counterpart may never disclose the information you need.

▲ Attitudes are more important than manners. Consequently, training should focus much more on value systems and challenging personal attitudes than on simply teaching the most appropriate greeting style. Superficial cultural training is not sufficient.

▲ Similar to negotiations, there is a time when the business deal is right.

▲ 'Making do' with the resources and adapting like a chameleon are necessary. This again shows an essential criterion of international managers: to leave their baggage and expectations behind and try to work with the situation they find rather than the one they wish to find.

▲ Getting the balance right between headquarters and periphery is also important. Again, this corresponds to intelligent career planning and the need to keep all parts informed, but possibly also the necessity to publicise one's achievements sufficiently and 'to let headquarters know'.

▲ Videoconferencing and modern communications technology can be helpful in reducing the number of business trips, but do we lose the opportunity to gauge customer mood? Business meetings have to be carefully planned, for example consideration needs to be given to what type of meetings have to be face to face.

Sir Win Bischoff, Chairman, Schroders

Educated at the University of the Witwatersrand, Johannesburg, obtained a BComm. Moved to New York to begin his career as a trainee with Chase Manhattan Bank and after two years joined J. Henry Schroder Wagg in London. In 1970 became Managing Director of Schroders & Chartered Ltd in Hong Kong. Returned to London with Schroders in 1983 and became Group Chief Executive a year later. A director of Schroders since 1983 and a director of J. Henry Schroder Wagg & Co since 1978. Chairman of Schroders plc since 1995, Chairman of Citigroup Europe, 2000.

Who is successful in international business?

"*People who are most successful are those who don't always think they are different; I have never thought of myself as different. The most important thing is to be yourself and to deal with people as you would always do. The challenge is really to make yourself not too different, you should not adapt to the extent that you make yourself forcibly too similar to the country you are operating in. The way you get there is to trust your instincts. You need to have a firm belief that the way you have been brought up gives you a sound base for judgment. There is a strong learning curve to get there.*

We already see a huge difference in the way companies employ international people, starting from graduate entries. The attitude of British businesspeople as well as Americans has changed – there is certainly a greater willingness to hire managers of other nationalities. For example, American managers are generally considered as pretty good.

Companies have to change their way of thinking – the thought process is expanding with the marketplace – it's more international. "

Mergers and acquisitions

"You have social architecture in any merger and acquisition whether it is mono-cultural or cross-cultural. One of the worst examples of cross-cultural mismanagement is when managers act against their stereotypes. This often upsets management situations. For example, when British managers try to behave like Americans in the US – this often causes a sense of confusion."

Bischoff left his native Germany at the age of 14. To my question about how he sees his own national/international identity after having moved around so much, he commented:

"Where the family is is where home is. When I lived in Hong Kong, home was there because of my family. I always suggest to my colleagues that they should see the foreign place they are working in as home. This is important, as it gives you a sense of belonging to a community and it also gets you involved in the local population much more. Since I have been living in Britain for about 15 years, I see myself as British."

International travel

"I usually travel once a week, mainly to Europe, with eight to nine trips to the US and six to the Far East per year. I do not have any special advice for frequent travelers. It's part of life. I wouldn't give anyone advice, as I see flying and traveling as so essential to business nowadays that one has automatically to accept them as necessities.

As to long-haul travel, different people do different things to cope with the physical demands. This ranges from eating nothing on the flight to having a special diet, etc. An international manager has to travel just as he has to learn how to manage others or fire people, which is painful. I have been lucky as I have always been excited by travel even as a young person and the excitement of travel never quite disappeared as I got older. It is certainly a question of attitude: a recent guest came straight from a transatlantic flight (the red-eye express) to lunch with me. When I admired him for being able to do this at the age of 82, he corrected me and said: 'You know I am 92 because you came to my 90th birthday party, not my 80th.' "

Mental preparation for international trips

"*If I know the language, for example German, I only read the language or discuss things in German on a trip to Germany. When I go to Italy, although I don't speak the language very well, I read the brief in English and then somebody gives me the translation. In this way, I pick up some of the essential words and issues in the language and then can 'switch on' in the discussion if it slips into Italian.*

I am not sure whether I would see myself as a strong linguist, but if I know the subject well, such as finance, I can learn and understand relatively quickly. I obviously speak English and German as well as Dutch and Afrikaans and I understand some Flemish, some French and a little Italian.

The way we prepare at Schroders is that we use our company resources very well: we always have briefing notes and discussions beforehand. I like to have a good idea about the strategy of the people I am meeting, their motivations and some knowledge of the country which I can use as a 'warm-up' conversation over lunch. "

Recruitment

What type of personality does he look for in recruits to his global management structure?

"*Sales personalities – obviously people also have to have management ability. Most of us can just about manage our secretaries as we have never been trained in management. With global expansion and products operating across regions, there is a stronger focus on personal adaptation. However, I believe one should not be overly adaptive. You have to have quite a firm attitude and be hard-headed in international business. If I have a mixed group of nine nationalities, I simply cannot adapt to all of those nationalities in a negotiation. I may, for example, agree with the Germans and the Americans but not necessarily with the Indonesians or Japanese. I have to weigh up whom I can upset or disagree with. One cannot be too relaxed in terms of adaptability but needs to take a clear direction.* **"**

Career planning

"*I have never had any career plan and in that sense I am an aberration. When I left school my father suggested that I should study economics and subsequently that I should go to law school in the US. My father also made the first banking contact for me at Chase Manhattan. When I came to London, I did not want to stay in normal banking and had the idea of merchant banking, but in those days I did not even take the trouble to learn about companies when going for interviews. This is certainly something that has changed nowadays.*

When I went to Schroders in Hong Kong, I was asked by someone I respected to go out there. At that time, I did not plan to go for a longer-term assignment as I was happy in London, with frequent trips to the US which I thoroughly enjoyed. I initially planned to stay in Hong Kong for about two years and ended up staying for twelve years.

As I have not managed my career consciously, I feel it is not right that I should give advice to others, but I would suggest the following:

▲ *It is important to have worked abroad, possibly for four to five years rather than just two to three. In my opinion, this longer time, particularly the last two years, gives you a real insight into the country or international business.*

▲ *Ideally, start working internationally when you are married. In that way, you can share your experience with your spouse even though the spouse may have to align her/his career to your own.* **"**

When I asked which personality characteristics made him really successful at international level, Bischoff answered rather modestly:

▲ *Fortuitous timing*
▲ *Right age*
▲ *Company needing some new input.*

Adaptation in Asia

"Overall, Asia was challenging because there was nothing when I started. It was a start-up operation but I would say I had a lot of luck.

After two years of living there, you feel that you know everybody, after five years you know that you do not know anybody well. You understand the importance of long-term relationships in terms of the Asian culture and the importance of not moving around too much. Only after five years do you know the relevant people and politics and the intricacies of the Chinese culture. Chinese culture is characterized by hard work, valuing education, loyalty to your friends and a strong relationship orientation. The Chinese want other people to owe them more than they owe you, so that in times of emergency or crises they can call on you. Another important consideration in this culture is to leave a profit for the next person. If you want a long-term relationship, you have to make sure that the negotiating partner is winning something and makes some profit. Otherwise, there is no incentive for him to continue the business relationship. You have to leave something. This is sometimes hard as a short-term orientation but in the long term it is a much better strategy.

In Asia, one also had to learn to understand that the family and family associations are very important and that there is a sense of obligation towards the extended family. "

The new international manager

"The new international manager is better educated technically in terms of management, has had management training, worked in a range of jobs and traveled. Nowadays, the business philosophy is much more towards open markets as opposed to protected markets. The American kind of open markets are paramount. "

Management literature

"I do not consciously go out and read management literature, but I have quite a number of colleagues with a Harvard background or people who read the strategic consultancy publications. We have a strong system of circulating relevant articles and I read about two to three management articles a week. There are about ten to twelve people who keep me abreast with new developments in this way. "

Commentary

▲ Win Bischoff's preparation for foreign trips in terms of languages is interesting. As most international business is conducted in English, the typical international manager assumes that this is the language needed to 'get by'. On most occasions this may be right. However, consider the advantage of having at least some understanding of a foreign language in picking up some of the key issues. Language skills can definitely give you an edge even if business is conducted in English.

▲ Although Bischoff did not really plan his career, he is an example of what most successful people do: he has the ability to listen to advice from senior executives, particularly those who act as mentors. This trust in senior executives' opinions as well as being flexible and taking on new tasks may still be a powerful combination in facilitating a career.

▲ In Bischoff's view, the ideal length of assignments is four to five years. This is an interesting point, particularly in view of the fact that most companies try to shorten international assignments to two years or less. Together with the increase in short-term projects and short-term international work, this call for longer-term assignments is in direct contrast to most management practices. Yet it is obvious that to achieve a real understanding of a foreign culture or market, one needs more than a couple of months – particularly in more complex jobs (joint ventures etc.), one only really becomes effective after a year or two.

▲ Adaptability should not be confused with lack of firmness in attitude and direction. Ultimately, success depends on international managers following a clear direction and being honest rather than on an extreme form of adaptation (as in changing one's opinion to whatever the situation is).

▲ Bischoff's approach to international work and adaptation is notable in that he likes to play down cultural differences. His view that adaptation is relatively straightforward may be influenced by his first experience of it at a relatively young age. At the age of 14, he went with his father to South Africa, a country whose language he did not speak. His mother, brothers and sisters followed a year later. After this early experience, any other transitions would have been much easier. His father also may have been a strong role model, as he had an international career working for IBM in the USA before moving to South Africa.

Edward Dolman, Group Chief Executive, Christie's

Read History at Southampton University and studied Fine and Decorative Arts before joining Christie's South Kensington in 1984. Main career steps: promoted to Director and Head of Furniture Department in 1990, Managing Director Christie's Amsterdam, 1996, Managing Director Christie's Europe (London) 1998, Managing Director US (New York) June 1999 and Group Chief Executive, December 1999.

Why did Christie's change to a global structure?

"We were only an international company in as much as we had operations in many countries. Most of the operations were independent entities and did not really work as one unified organization. The new structure creates one organization representing different countries.

Clients do business across country borders and it was really a client-driven decision to internationalize our structure. Otherwise, we would have faced a situation where a client in Germany was happy to deal with the German, Paris, London or New York operation and the independence of these auction centers could have led to massive competition within the business. The new structure allows a much better global service to our clients.

The first step was to create a business plan that focused on globalization and this was discussed and agreed by the senior management team of the company. The next step was to develop a detailed organizational plan and structure for the new global company meeting the aims in the new business plan. We then took back this organizational plan to the senior management and discussed the necessary organizational changes to achieve globalization.

At that stage, the buy-in was not complete because of some of the harsher consequences of globalization. For example, it was clear that some individuals' positions would change and we therefore needed to discuss this further to get the final buy-in. The ultimate aim was to retain our employees and it was important to change the structure in a sensitive way – we needed to keep our key people and offer them exciting alternative roles. It took about 12 months from the strategic conception to starting to implement the new organizational plan.

The next stage was obviously getting the troops on the ground to replicate the process. We had to communicate the plans and principles to everyone and we had to communicate quickly all the organizational changes that needed to be made. This also resulted in changing individuals' reporting lines and structure.

The acceptance of the new structure was fairly predictable. People who were not directly affected by the organizational change, or in some cases benefited from the change, were happy. Where jobs were affected and in some cases disappeared, employees obviously objected. But it was interesting that this was not necessarily because of the personal effect, but because they often could not believe that the role was not important any more when elements of their role were, in fact, redistributed to other roles.

Redundancy was not ever a real threat in this reorganization. Great care was taken to find alternative positions. **"**

A global mindset

"Before our globalization, everyone was focused on the bottom-line performance of their own region, which meant that all the individual activities were concentrated on the final goal of improving the profits for their particular center. As a consequence, there was not sufficient regard for the international health of the company. There was too much incentive to keep clients and profits at a local level. Now, we have changed this dramatically by having one global profit center guaranteeing that we are even more client focused and that we will be in a position of moving properties much more between countries, which will ultimately help clients. One would also expect that this will make it much more interesting for our employees.

In the past, the management technique was to take a very insular view and to present being too international as a 'risk'. We have *changed this around in trying to make people see the opportunities that are gained with a more international mindset. But still, one has to recognize that some people prefer to be a 'big fish in a small pond'. The mindset now is 'wait and see' and, ultimately, we have to demonstrate the benefits of the reorganization for the next step of employee buy-in.*

I can certainly say that, from a senior management perspective, the reorganization has been very successful, which we can see in the ability to manage the company in a much faster way. For example, before the new structure, policies could not be implemented company wide but always had to be adapted and agreed at local level, which was a long-winded and sometimes inefficient process. Now, with operational standards being controlled centrally, best-practice approaches to business processes can be implemented much more easily.

An example is the development of our data system for valuations for clients. This is obviously a key information system for us. In the old structure, to implement this system, you would have to go to each local unit to get approval and after months of communicating with the regional centers, there would only be partial take-up. Now, we can introduce the new system in one meeting. This is just a simple example. Other examples include the international standards and organization of catalogs, i.e. to make them uniform around the world. ""

The auction business

"*The process of internationalization at Christie's is similar to many other industry sectors, but I think the auction business is quite unique. We are dealing with very high-value, totally subjective assessments, in markets that fluctuate widely, and it is difficult to think of true parallels in other business sectors. An old master picture is worth $15 million or $500,000 million depending on the valuation of two or three experts. It depends on the quality of the experts and the way the expert can influence the market. The business is high risk, with high returns but also high losses. For example, a Van Gogh may have been worth $1 million* *in 1986, but one year later it would be worth $12 million, and three years later $36 million.* "

The influence of the internet

"*It is interesting to consider that our organizational change was also driven by the internet. First of all, obviously, we reviewed our general internet strategy in the auction business. But also, at a more operational level, we needed to present Christie's as one unified company on the web and not as many different companies in different regions.*

We could not have catalogs differently priced or presented any more – we needed uniform processes. The standardization of processes and catalogs has also helped us to make savings in IT.

Our strategy toward the internet is to add value but not to change the basic auction process. We will concentrate on our traditional business and believe we will attract more people to it via the internet, which is now much more interactive. We have art experts or artists speaking on the web. Obviously, potential buyers can get information on sales and they can also bid over the internet. "

The effect of email on international management

"*Email and the internet are incredibly useful tools for gathering information, but also incredibly bad management tools for communication. In multicultural organizations, the misunderstanding that emails can cause is unbelievable. For example, if an email is simply translated from French into English, it can come across as confrontational. English translated into Dutch is seen as misleading and deceitful. Different words carry different meanings in different languages. I therefore see email as a prime cause of miscommunication at the international level.*

I believe in people picking up the phone and speaking to each other. I do think email has benefits in terms of disseminating information, but in the true sense of communication it is very unhelpful. You need to have face-to-face meetings. Email also sometimes messes up people's sense of priority. Because email is fast, our instinct is often to reply to emails quickly, and there are also managers who will vilify staff if they don't respond fast enough. Email often takes precedence in executives' lives, but it is a false prioritization. "

What helped him become leader of a global organization?

"*I think I was reasonably well prepared for the job. I have always been interested in motivating people and in working in teams.*

I showed this interest early on, when I organized all the sports teams at school and university, in rugby and cricket. I was captain of many teams and learnt a lot about what bonded teams together and what destroyed them. A lot of my management style is really based on this early experience.

I am very intolerant of poor performance – I believe that one team member's poor performance is destructive for the entire team. Take the example of a highly motivated soccer team coming to training three times a week. If the center forward never hits the goal, the rest of the team becomes completely demotivated and you can see the standards and morale of the rest of the team drop dramatically.

If you want to motivate people effectively, you have to look at some essential drivers. It is not cash that motivates people, it is status, recognition, an understanding of what job they are performing and what their value-added role is in the organization. If these ingredients are not there, you cannot get high performance out of employees.

In terms of international management, I had my watershed experience when I was promoted to Managing Director of Christie's in Amsterdam. It was my first non-UK managerial experience and I think it prepared me well for a larger role. I found the cultural differences between the Netherlands and the UK enormous. One should not underestimate cultural differences, even in Europe. If you think the Dutch work environment is the same as the English or the French, you are completely mistaken. My work in Amsterdam helped me realize how different people are and how these differences are formed by language, religion and general values.

In communication style, for example, the Dutch prefer a

brutally honest and direct conversation and feel uncomfortable if they cannot get it. They therefore think that the vague or indirect approach of the British is rather conceited. The British in turn think the Dutch are plain rude. Another example is that the British sometimes have a false sense of security with Americans because of the common language. "

Transition from European Managing Director to Global CEO

"The main change was from being hands-on and knowing what's happening everywhere to being much more isolated and working over a big distance and therefore managing by remote control. I know that I get much more diffuse messages because I simply cannot be in all offices finding out exactly what is going on. It is in a way more difficult to get high-quality information or to know what the real tone is and, of course, the general level of responsibility has grown dramatically. "

Personality characteristics

"I have a firm belief and confidence in what I am doing. I am not easily defeated and I take as much advice as I can, but once I have all of the information and get good feedback from others around me, I make the decision.

I am seen as someone who has good interpersonal skills and who is approachable. This means that people feel they can say controversial things to me and explore things, without the risk of being heavily criticized. I do not play political games and try to stay even-handed, but the leadership issue is absolutely key for an organization: you need to care about your employees and have an understanding approach to people who work for you. "

Commentary

▲ Christie's globalization shows many parallels with the globalization of companies in other industry sectors. Globalization requires a consistent and coordinated approach along three lines: the business strategy, the organizational structure and employee buy-in. The process at Christie's also shows the long timeframe in achieving globalization, particularly in developing a global mindset. Many organizations ask external consultants for help in developing their employees' international mindsets. However, the same organizations often don't have the necessary structures in place to support a global mindset, such as global profit centers.

▲ The effects of the internet and email on international management have hardly been researched at present. Previous research has shown that email generally reduces inhibitions and therefore often results in hasty, emotional and badly thought-through communication. The intercultural miscommunication to which Edward Dolman refers supports this. Moreover, it illustrates again that English as a global language is not used and understood in the same way by people of different cultural backgrounds and can lead to enormous misunderstandings.

▲ It is also interesting to consider that email may give us a completely wrong sense of priorities in business situations.

▲ Dolman's comments on leadership mirror the characteristics of the new global leader: a team-oriented, non-political approach, involving others and taking a genuine interest in the opinions and the well-being of employees. This is diametrically opposite to the old model of authoritarian, hierarchical and quite political leadership. Most importantly, the message is never to underestimate cross-cultural differences.

▲ International business requires resilience and the ability to get up and start again. Things go wrong in new and relatively unpredictable situations, and global leaders often comment on having experienced some failures in cross-cultural business situations. One needs the emotional robustness of not being easily defeated, a strong belief in one's abilities, and general perseverance.

Diversity of boards

In recent years, discussions concerning company boards in many countries have been dominated by issues of corporate governance and executive pay. Research has focused on changes in board practices and comparative salaries of top executives. Less is known about the board composition of international companies and there is little information on one of the most important questions: do the most admired companies have different kinds of board? Is there a relationship between board composition and company reputation?

This was the main objective of one of my studies: to find out whether the boards of Britain's most reputable and admired companies have any unique characteristics. The fifteen most admired companies (as defined by an independent study and criteria, and including companies such as Glaxo Wellcome, BP, GKN and Reuters) were compared with the 'rest' of the top 100 companies in the UK with regard to board composition. The findings suggest a connection between board composition and company reputation.

The most admired companies show a more diverse board composition in terms of gender, international experience and early career background. They have boards with a slightly higher number of female directors, directors have more international experience, are better educated and come from a wider range of professional and functional backgrounds. It is logical to assume that more diverse boards will be better equipped to deal with the complexities of today's business.

Obviously, more studies are needed to investigate the causal relationship between board composition and company performance. However, it seems that today's criteria for board-level searches are certainly heading in the right direction. Search companies are more and more frequently asked to find executives with international experience or of different nationalities for the boards of large companies to cover the diversity of their markets. This is particularly evident in the search for CEOs and chairmen. One *Sunday Times* survey showed that 40 percent of CEOs and chairmen of Britain's top 100 companies were of foreign nationality, including CK Chow, the Hong Kong

Chinese CEO of GKN; Marjorie Scardino, the American CEO of Pearson; and Allen Yurko, the American CEO of Invensys. In 1997, Americans dominated the 'foreign CEO/chairmen list' of the 100 largest companies in Britain.

Virtual teams

One of the challenges of global business is managing virtual teams – teams not only composed of different nationalities but of people who work from remote locations all over the world, coordinating their efforts to achieve global results. As a by-product of the internet revolution, there has been a dramatic increase in this kind of team.

The experience of Syzygy – a consultancy and development company in the eservices sector – illustrates some of the issues of virtual teams.

A pan-European ebusiness solutions provider, Syzygy helps to accelerate 'bricks and mortar' companies into becoming profitable ebusinesses. With a management board of UK and German executives, Syzygy was originally formed through a merger of UK, French and German companies. It is fast growing and presently employs about 200 people throughout Europe. CEO Chris Robson describes the two main challenges of remote management as the need to find a shared business vision and values, and the challenge of solving problems without being face to face.

> " *Although we had clear expectations of what the drivers of success would be when we merged the three companies, we spent a lot of time defining what our 'new' brand and business are about and in trying to distill our core values. We are still in the process of this and it has taken us about eight months to come to a solid and shared level of brand identity. Differences in vision and values are not really an issue any more at senior management level. We have a consistent view of life, but the next challenge is to create a consistent view further down the organization. A large part of our business is pan-European and is carried out in our cross-country project teams. This provides the opportunity to ensure that the vision is brought to life practically for people*

through real client business. Accordingly, we have spent consider-
able time examining how to build teams that believe in and follow
our overall goals.

With regard to the second issue, I try to convince people to use
the phone rather than email to solve problems. Email is excellent
for circulating information, but as a problem-solving tool it is not
efficient. It is ultimately not good for resolving arguments or for
having a real debate. Communicating by phone or face-to-face
meeting is dramatically better than paper or email.

We also had to deal with many cross-cultural differences. The
Germans tend to be more formal and precise about life, whereas
the British and the French are often less precise and more hypo-
thetical, which can cause enormous frustrations.

Also, there are very different views about creativity. The French
and the British love debating, whereas the Germans debate less
and really want to come up with a plan of action quickly.

But these are relatively small issues. Altogether, I find it
extremely exciting to run a pan-European group, as our industry
attracts smart people, making it worth overcoming some of the
obstacles on the way. **"**

An example of a virtual team working between New York and London may illustrate some of these challenges as well as approaches to
overcoming potential difficulties.

Originally, two teams from this American worldwide organization
focused on the European and US markets respectively. In a move to
globalize their services, the teams were asked to coordinate their
efforts much more closely to facilitate better client development and
more effective transactions. This included more cross-border deals
and increased communication via email and videoconferencing.

I was asked to help this team maximize its strengths and increase
its already excellent business performance. The specific aims were:

▲ Improved communication. Ideally, team members needed to talk
   to each other more and collaborate more closely.
▲ Better understanding of cultural differences in communication.
   There were strong cross-cultural differences between doing
   business in London and in New York. Additionally, the teams

comprised different nationalities.
▲ Agreement on group behavior and expectations. Team members
   varied enormously on what they expected of each other, i.e. there
   were no clear rules.

A pre-development questionnaire identified these critical areas:

▲ Collaboration was patchy.
▲ Team members were too competitive and some tried to outshine
   their colleagues or, in the worst case, act against them.
▲ There was a lack of respect.
▲ Geographic differences were seen as a dividing factor.
▲ Get-togethers were infrequent and formal.
▲ People were still working in 'silos', not as a group.
▲ Other problems included distrust and back-stabbing.

Overall, there was a failure to recognize sufficiently the global nature
of the business. In a way, it was a classic scenario where two successful teams, consisting of highly ambitious and somewhat individualistic executives, understood rationally the need to operate globally, but
emotionally and behaviorally were not quite ready for it.

Approach to team development

Individual management development sessions (oriented toward an
assessment of international effectiveness and styles) provided the basis
of a summary team report. Each individual team member participated
in a six-hour assessment and feedback session, which was primarily
geared at their own development and covered topics such as:

▲ Communication style and relationship skills (assertiveness, people orientation versus self-sufficiency, sensitivity, need for recognition, need for autonomy, need for leadership).
▲ Task approach and working style (careful versus enthusiastic,
   structured versus flexible, realistic versus implications oriented,
   pragmatic versus strategic).
▲ Ability to deal with stress.

▲ Cross-cultural awareness and sensitivity.
▲ Career values

All individual reports were summarized into a team report, which formed the basis for the subsequent team development. The report analyzed the strengths and weaknesses of the team and potential risks in relation to their business strategy.

Main findings

The results showed an extremely interesting, mixed picture. On the positive side, the team had high task orientation and an experimental, entrepreneurial outlook, which were positive for developing new business ideas. However, the team was also highly competitive, probably explaining the amount of in-fighting and also increasing the risk of having a 'culture of blame'.

The high self-sufficiency of individual members obviously made it difficult to develop a more team-oriented approach. The team also had a strong need for structure, indicating a lack of flexibility and an inability to accept other ways of doing things. A by-product of the high task orientation was a lack of interpersonal sensitivity, i.e. team members were not attuned to what was going on with other people. These characteristics obviously had a negative impact on international effectiveness in relation to clients, but also transatlantic collaboration.

Moreover, there were distinct cultural differences between New York and London. The New York team was much more extrovert, socially bold, structured and stronger on leadership and self-confidence. This obviously created the risk of New York dominating London and resulted in tensions. Most interestingly, despite the success of the team, the psychological data indicated that its members needed a stronger external focus. Its internal tensions distracted the team from concentrating on the competition and developing new clients.

Team session and follow-up

A one-day workshop formed the basis for ongoing team development. The workshop started with a framework for successful teams, presented the overall team results and their implications, and split the team results into London–New York groups to illustrate some of the cultural differences. The workshop and ongoing follow-up concentrated on collaboration and communication issues and developed concrete action plans to work on basic team values and external orientation.

Examples of externally oriented initiatives included new product development and reviewing the research and development strategy. Team members also agreed on the basic rules and improvement of their own behavior and committed to follow these through. Special projects were assigned that were coordinated by individual team members over the course of the next six months.

Pre- and post-workshop measurements of team effectiveness suggested that the team worked much better after the intervention: there are fewer complaints about problems and communication has improved. Most importantly, the company's global business performance has improved significantly.

10

Are You an Effective International Manager?

The aim of this chapter is to help you reflect on some of the issues that are important for success in international work. It does not matter if you are just about to embark on an assignment, if you have recently returned from a spell abroad or if you are in the middle of one. It is also applicable to those working in international teams and with multinational business partners.

The exercise gives insight into how easy it is for you to be successful, how much you will enjoy international work and what areas you may have to be careful about or may have to develop. A discussion of some of the factors at the end of the chapter will help you evaluate your responses, but for now, I suggest you run through all of the questions and write down your answers in the spaces provided.

The areas considered are:

▲ the culture shock triangle, followed by
▲ personality characteristics for the self-assessment (see Figure 9).

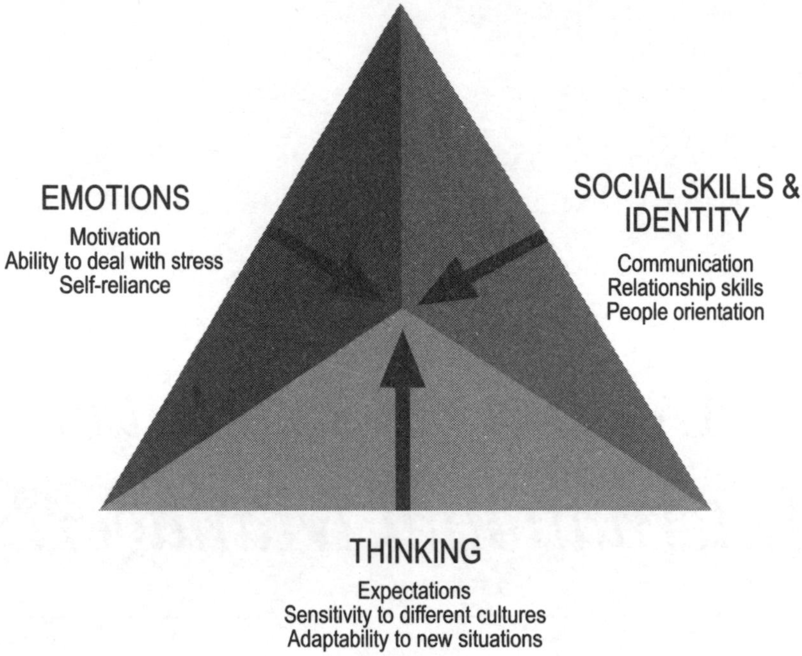

EMOTIONS
Motivation
Ability to deal with stress
Self-reliance

SOCIAL SKILLS &
IDENTITY

Communication
Relationship skills
People orientation

THINKING
Expectations
Sensitivity to different cultures
Adaptability to new situations

Figure 9 Personality characteristics and the culture shock triangle

Motivation

Describe your main motivation for international work.

How much is your motivation determined by:

❏ Opportunity to take a major career step and accept more responsibility

❏ Desire to learn something new

❏ Wish to progress fast in my career

❏ Excitement of living abroad

❏ Opportunity for spouse and family

❏ Wish to become more international, i.e. more culturally aware and socially skilled

❏ Enjoying a more comfortable lifestyle

❏ The company insisting/forcing me to go

❏ Wanting to make large amounts of money (as the prime reason)

❏ Saving a rocky relationship with spouse/partner by having a change of environment

❏ Escaping a difficult work situation in home country (e.g. company restructuring, power struggles, personality clashes)

❐ Wanting to show the 'locals' in X how to run a business

❐ Not really interested in international work but see it as an absolute must if I want to get ahead

❐ Getting out of a rut

Expectations

What do you think are the main differences in working and/or living in X, compared to your home country? (Try to think of several.)

What will you miss most and how can you compensate for it?

What would be the advantages of your going to X and what would be the disadvantages?

What would be the ideal scenario for your move to X?

What would be the worst scenario?

How can you achieve the ideal scenario?

How can you prevent the worst scenario?

Personality

It is impossible to assess personality characteristics in a reliable way with a few questions. Nevertheless, it may be useful to consider the following dimensions yourself and check your view with your manager, boss or spouse in order to 'get a feel' for your personality. The following areas are those most often assessed in relation to international assignments.

Sensitivity to different cultures

How much interest in foreign cultures have you shown in the past?

❏ Foreign travel?

❏ Books and reading?

❏ Foreign friends?

❏ Interest in international business?

How much knowledge do you have about different cultures?

❏ In-depth knowledge of which cultures?

❏ Superficial knowledge of which cultures?

How would you gauge your tolerance level?

❏ In which situations have you shown a lot of tolerance?

❏ In which situations have you shown very little tolerance?

Adaptability to new situations

How do you generally react in unpredictable/ambiguous situations?

How flexible (e.g. different approaches, changing procedures, modifying schedules) do you consider yourself to be?

What languages do you speak? (well/moderately/basic)

Communication/relationship skills/people orientation

How would you describe your interpersonal style? Are you assertive, quiet, dominant?

Are you more introvert or extravert? Would you rather spend time by yourself or socializing with others?

Are you shy/reserved or more adventurous in unfamiliar social situations? How easy do you find it to make contact with new people?

How easy is it for you to be empathic and understand others?

What is your management style and how easy is it for you to adapt your style? Are you autocratic/directive or more team oriented and democratic?

What do you think is the impact on others of your current interpersonal and working style?

Ability to deal with stress

Have you had any stress-related problems in the past and what have you done about them?

How do you react under pressure?

How easy is it for you to deal with a large number of changes? Think about comparable changes in the past (like moving house, changing jobs etc.).

Self-reliance

Make a list of situations in the past where you have shown the ability to make decisions independently and exhibited self-reliance, particularly under adverse circumstances.

Evaluation of the self-assessment

Motivation

Motivation can be both positive and negative. Your motivation influences the way you adapt internationally. Positive motivation means curiosity about the new culture, excitement at working abroad, wanting a new challenge, the urge to become more global. Negative motivation occurs where we want to make more money and nothing else, or where we want to escape a difficult situation. The latter are clearly scenarios that are not ideal for taking on an international assignment and there is evidence that negative motivation and failure go hand in hand.

Expectations

Look back at your expectations in an objective way. Consider whether they are specific enough, whether you have thought sufficiently about what it will be like to live and work in the new place, how much you depend on the comforts of your own country and whether you have given enough consideration to the advantages and disadvantages of taking on the assignment, both for yourself and your family.

Personality

▲ If your answers show that your *sensitivity to different cultures* may not be very high, do more reading, try to meet nationals of that country and find out about its history, politics and management style.

▲ If you come to the conclusion that you do not deal well with *unpredictable and ambiguous situations*, and that those situations make you very edgy, you may seriously consider not taking on a long-term international assignment, but start with short-term projects. Alternatively, think of ways of reducing your reaction to stress in such situations (learning to accept that not everything can be 100 percent planned and that intercultural situations are not clear cut).

▲ If you have been described as *inflexible in relation to schedules and procedures* and you are going to a place where schedules and deadlines are handled differently to what you are used to, it is important to think about how you can relax from a highly schedule-driven approach. How can you encourage yourself to be more flexible?

▲ Learning even the basics of the *language* of the country in which you will be living can give you different insights into the society and help you achieve rapport faster with your host-country nationals. In addition, when you are using your own language, be careful not to use too many idioms and consider the relevance of your sense of humor.

▲ If you are shy and reserved, how can you establish *social contacts*, particularly in a business setting? In many cultures, business and social relationships are intertwined. The trick is to develop a style that is comfortable for you but also effective in business and social relationships.

▲ If you are not sure about your *management style* and how you appear to other people, ask your colleagues or your boss. Get a clear idea of what you do before inflicting it on foreign colleagues!

▲ If you have had *stress-related problems* in the past, it is best to talk to an expert about stress-management techniques and how you can reduce the stresses that usually come with international assignments.

▲ People have varying degrees of *self-reliance*: some love the opportunity to be highly independent and not having to report

back to headquarters too often, whereas others are positively
frightened by the idea. On whatever end of the scale you find
yourself, it is useful to think about whether you can deal with the
independence inherent in international assignments and how you
will establish rapport with headquarters. If you are not very self-
reliant but you still want to go and the company still wants to
send you, how can you set up a network that will help make you
feel more comfortable?

Bibliography

Alston, E. and Stratford, R. (1996) How children cope with relocation: methodological concerns in the study of mobility and its effect on children. Paper presented at the *British Psychological Conference*, London.

Barham, K. and Oates, D. (1993) *The International Manager*. London: Pitman Publishing.

Beck, A.T. (1967) *Depression: Clinical, Experimental and Theoretical Aspects*. New York: Hoeber.

Bond, M.H. (ed.) (1986) *The Psychology of the Chinese People*. Oxford: Oxford University Press.

Brewster, C. (1991) *The Management of Expatriates*. London: Kogan Page.

Campbell, N. (1996) *European Expatriates in China*. Manchester: China Research Unit, Manchester Business School.

Deal, T. and Kennedy, A. (1982) *Corporate Cultures*. Reading, MA: Addison Wesley.

Dohrenwend, B.P. and Dohrenwend, B.S. (1974) *Stressful Life Events: Their Nature and Effects*. New York: John Wiley.

D'Zurilla, T.J. and Goldfried, M.R. (1971). Problem solving and behaviour modification. *Journal of Abnormal Psychology*, 78: 107–26.

Forster, N. (1993) International job mobility and relocation in the 1990s. *European Work and Organisational Psychologist*, 2 (3): 191.

Friedman, M. and Rosenman, R.H. (1969) The possible general causes of coronary artery disease. In M. Friedman (ed.) *Pathogenesis of Coronary Artery Disease*. New York: McGraw-Hill.

Furnham, A. and Bochner, S. (1986) *Culture Shock*. London: Routledge.

Gertsen, M.C. (1990) Intercultural competence and expatriates. *International Journal of Human Resource Management*, 1 (3): 341–62.

Goleman, D. (1996) *Emotional Intelligence*. London: Bloomsbury.

Hall, E. and Hall, M.R. (1990) *Understanding Cultural Differences*. Yarmouth: Intercultural Press.

Hampden-Turner, C. and Trompenaars, F. (1993) *The Seven Cultures of Capitalism*. London: Piatkus.

Harré, R. and Parrott, W.G. (1996) *Emotions: the Social, Cultural and Physical Dimensions*. London: Sage.

Hawes, F. and Kealey (1981). Canadians in development: an empirical study of Canadian technical assistants. *International Journal of Intercultural Relations*, 5: 239–58.

Hofstede, G. (1994) *Cultures and Organisations*. London: HarperCollins.

Johnson, M. (1998) *Building and Retaining Global Talent: Towards 2002*. London: Economist Intelligence Unit.

Lazarus, R.S. (1966) *Psychological Stress and the Coping Process*. New York: McGraw-Hill.

Lazarus, R.S. and Folkman, S. (1984) *Stress, Appraisal and Coping*. New York: Springer.

Marx, E. (1996a) *The International Manager*. London: NB Selection.

Marx, E. (1996b) *International Human Resource Practices in the UK and Germany*. London: Anglo-German Foundation.

Marx, E (1996c) *The Move to the Top*. London: NB Selection.

Marx, E. (1998) *Symptoms of Culture Shock*. London: NB Selection/Centre for Intercultural Briefing.

Marx, E. and Demby, N. (1998) *Grooming for the Board*. London: NB Selection/Arthur Andersen.

Mole, J. (1995) *Mind Your Manners*. London: Nicholas Brealey.

Oberg, K. (1960) Culture shock: adjustment to new cultural environments. *Practical Anthropology*, 7: 177–82.

Ratin, I. (1983) Thinking internationally: a comparison of how international executives learn. *International Studies of Management and Organisation*, 13 (1–2): 139–50.

van Ruitenbeek, D. (1998) The expatriate psychological contract. Conference presentation, *SIETAR*.

Schoenberg, R.J. (1997). The impact of management style differences on the performance of European cross-border acquisitions. Unpublished doctoral thesis, Imperial College, University of London.

Seligman, M.E.P. (1975) *Helplessness*. San Francisco: Freeman.

Seligman, M.E.P. and Schulman, P. (1986). Explanatory style as a predictor of productivity and quitting among life insurance agents. *Journal of Personality and Social Psychology*, 50: 832–38.

Shell International (1993) *Outlook – Expatriate Survey*.

Stoner, J.A.F., Aram, J.D. and Rubin, J. (1972) Factors associated with effective performance in overseas work assignments. *Personnel Psychology*, 25: 303–18.

Torbiörn, I. (1982) *Living Abroad: Personal Adjustment and Personnel Policy in the Overseas Setting*. Chichester: John Wiley.

Trompenaars, F. and Hampden-Turner, C. (1997) *Riding the Waves of Culture*. London: Nicholas Brealey.

Wilkinson, J. (1989) Expatriate Families in Asia. Cranfield School of Management, HRRC working paper (unpublished).

Index